高校英语选修课系列教材

# VOICING CHINA
## Through Public Speaking

# 新英语
# 演讲教程

总主编 李 昀
主 编 荣 榕
编 者 李 昀
　　　　屈 薇
　　　　荣 榕
　　　　[澳] 安德鲁·克罗科姆（Andrew Crocombe）

清華大学出版社
北京

## 内 容 简 介

本教程以英语演讲技能训练为抓手,以介绍中国实现联合国可持续发展目标(SDGs)的道路、方案和智慧为导线,引领学生运用公共演讲技巧系统地向世界介绍改革开放以来,中国在落实扶贫攻坚、健康福祉、清洁能源、公平公正、气候行动、维护和平、城市可持续发展和倡导人类命运共同体等方面取得的令世界瞩目的成就。本教程强调真实场景的模拟训练,特意增加了知识激活、技能实践、自我反思、情景演讲任务、基于任务学习等板块,把协作调研、项目规划等融入演讲设计,引导学生在思考、实践和社会中学习如何向世界介绍中国。

版权所有,侵权必究。举报:010-62782989,beiqinquan@tup.tsinghua.edu.cn。

图书在版编目(CIP)数据

新英语演讲教程 / 李昀总主编;荣榕主编. —北京:清华大学出版社,2023.1
高校英语选修课系列教材
ISBN 978-7-302-62534-6

Ⅰ. ①新… Ⅱ. ①李… ②荣… Ⅲ. ①英语—演讲—高等学校—教材 Ⅳ. ① H311.9

中国国家版本馆 CIP 数据核字(2023)第 017553 号

责任编辑:白周兵
封面设计:子 一
责任校对:王凤芝
责任印制:曹婉颖

出版发行:清华大学出版社
　　　　　网　　址:http://www.tup.com.cn, http://www.wqbook.com
　　　　　地　　址:北京清华大学学研大厦 A 座　　邮　编:100084
　　　　　社 总 机:010-83470000　　邮　购:010-62786544
　　　　　投稿与读者服务:010-62776969, c-service@tup.tsinghua.edu.cn
　　　　　质量反馈:010-62772015, zhiliang@tup.tsinghua.edu.cn
印 装 者:北京同文印刷有限责任公司
经　　销:全国新华书店
开　　本:185mm×260mm　　印　张:10.5　　字　数:211 千字
版　　次:2023 年 2 月第 1 版　　印　次:2023 年 2 月第 1 次印刷
定　　价:59.00 元

产品编号:096166-01

# 前言

党的二十大提出,中国式现代化创造人类文明新形态,为人类实现现代化提供新选择。用中国理念造福人类,让更多中国人参与国际事务,是中国参与全球治理、贡献全球发展、为人类谋进步、为世界谋大同的重要途径。然而,长期以来,由于公共话题讨论、公共演讲和公共辩论能力在我国整个教育体系中培养不足,我们参与国际事务的人才有所欠缺,不利于我们运用中国智慧、中国方案、中国力量为世界之问、时代之问寻找答案。而外语教育中中国话题的不足,也致使我们的学生在国际交流中缺少介绍中国经验的意识和能力,影响了中国道路在国际的传播。如何培养一批兼具家国情怀、国际视野和国际竞争力的全球治理人才,已经成为外语教育亟待解决的问题。

因此,本教程以联合国 17 个可持续发展目标为蓝本,将课程思政融入广泛的英语语言能力培养中,引导学生学习如何运用公共演讲技巧,向世界介绍中国现代化进程中取得的新成就,以及在落实扶贫攻坚、健康福祉、清洁能源、公平公正、气候行动、维护和平、城市可持续发展和倡导人类命运共同体等方面积累的新智慧,助力学生积极参与国际公共话题的讨论、辩论与演讲,与时俱进。

## 教程编写理念

与传统英语演讲教材重技巧轻内容、重语言轻思想、重西方文化讨论轻中国智慧传播不同,本教程立足本土,放眼世界,充分展示当代中国在诸多国际关注领域取得的成就,让学生在听、说、读、写、辩中深入了解中国的发展,展开讨论中国方案给全人类共同发展带来的启示,促进学生知识、能力、素质协调发展,激发他们的爱国热情,拓展他们的国际视野。

这样的理念也需要教学方法的改革向实践能力偏斜。本教程采用体验式英语演讲学习方式,引导学生在真实的国际交流场景中,灵活运用英语演讲技巧,完成富有挑战性的真实演讲任务,通过创造沉浸式、调研式和合作式的学习体验,多方调动学生的学习积极性、主动性和参与性,提升他们的批判性思维能力、自我反思能力和团队合作精神，帮助他们领会公共演讲的精髓。

## 教程特色

相比其他英语演讲教材，本教程的突出特色在于：

### 1. 演讲话题价值引领

本教程各单元的演讲主题以认识、理解和传播中国智慧为核心，紧扣联合国可持续发展目标，选取最新时事素材，把中国智慧，尤其是解决当前国际社会共同面对的问题的方案融入演讲设计；在培养学生认识、理解和反思各类公共话题的同时，提升其运用英语演讲技巧，有效讲述中国故事、传播中国智慧的能力。

### 2. 理论实践密切结合

本教程共分十个单元，每单元内部一讲一练。演讲内容上，一个单元围绕一个联合国可持续发展目标展开深入讨论；演讲技巧上，前六个单元紧扣演讲单项技能训练，后四个单元转向整体把握，通过整合练习，帮助学生温故知新，充分调动前六个单元所学，完成整合性演讲设计和演练。每个单元的总结部分设计有完整的情景演讲任务，内容与形式、理论与实践紧密结合，让学生学以致用，学用相长。

### 3. 活动设计多元立体

围绕单元内容和演讲技巧，本教程设计了全新的教学活动，针对中国学生缺乏公共话题讨论和真实场景公共演讲的问题，在普通演讲教材的基础上，特别增加了知识激活、技能实践、自我反思、情景演讲任务、基于任务学习等板块，把协作调研、项目规划等融入演讲设计。此外，本教程还在单元末的练习中提供了联合国关于各个目标的说明，方便学生查阅，引导学生在思考中学、在实践中学、在社会中学，尤其是在形式多样的演讲实训中学会自我评估、自我纠正和自我提升。

### 4. 形式编排新颖实用

在编排形式上，本教程紧跟时代，摒弃传统教材的长篇说教，把内容和指令图表化、视觉化和简洁化，并配以简明的英语解说，减少阅读障碍，有利于学生把更多的时间用于演讲技能和内容设计的学习上，优化教学过程。此外，本教程还在智慧树平台同步开放了MOOC课程"英语演讲"，便于学生学习和观摩，提升教学质量。

## 使用说明

本教程在设计上充分考虑了21世纪人才培养需求，可用于高校英语专业、大学英语、双语通识课以及国际组织人才集训类的教学。教师在具体使用过程中，应充分考虑演讲技巧与内容表达的结合：在演讲技巧方面，注重讲练结合，让学生在技能学习后，立即投入实操，把握演讲技能的综合运用，并鼓励学生在单元复习中自查自改；在演讲内容方面，紧扣每单元的情景演讲任务，鼓励学生通过知识激活、问题调研和设计合作，在深入了解相关信息和素材的基础上，设计出可以揭示中国道路、显露中国智慧的演讲方案，并模拟真实演讲情景，进行实战演练。

在实际教学过程中，教师可根据教学目标、学生水平、专业背景、地域特征等具体情况，灵活选取教材与慕课内容，鼓励学生结合实践，立体多层地组织自己的演讲，增加教学的趣味性、丰富性和灵活性。

**编写团队**

本教程汇集了华南理工大学、中山大学、暨南大学、华南师范大学、广东外语外贸大学、河海大学等多所高校的优秀教师团队，他们对本教程进行了精心的编撰和审稿，使之具有一定的科学性、规范性和先进性。然而，时代变化日新月异，中国理念也在不断发展，我们欢迎各位专家、教师和学生在教学和使用过程中提出宝贵意见和建议，帮助更新和完善本教程。

编者

2022 年 7 月

# Contents

## Unit 1 — Introducing Public Speaking   1
- 1.1   What Is Public Speaking?   3
- 1.2   How Does "Being in Public" Affect Your Speaking?   4
- 1.3   How to Be a Responsible Public Speaker?   7
- 1.4   How to Speak More Confidently?   10
- 1.5   Final Questions   11

**Final Speech Topic**

Sustainable Development Goal 12: Responsible Consumption and Production   11

## Unit 2 — Analyzing the Audience   15
- 2.1   What Is Audience Demographics?   17
- 2.2   What Are Audience Culture and Stereotyping?   20
- 2.3   What Do You Know About the Audience's Psychology, and How Can You Use It?   21
- 2.4   How to Find Out More About the Audience?   22
- 2.5   Final Questions   25

**Final Speech Topic**

Sustainable Development Goal 11: Sustainable Cities and Communities   25

## Unit 3 — Designing Topics and Purposes   29
- 3.1   Why Do You Need a Topic and Purposes for Your Speech?   31
- 3.2   How Can You Choose a Really Good Topic?   33
- 3.3   How to Narrow Down a Topic?   39
- 3.4   General Purpose, Specific Purpose & Thesis Statement   40
- 3.5   Final Questions   43

**Final Speech Topic**

Sustainable Development Goal 3: Good Health and Well-being   44

## Unit 4: Using Supporting Information   47

- **4.1** What Is Supporting Information and Why Is It Important?   49
- **4.2** What Kinds of Supporting Information Are There?   51
- **4.3** Where to Find Supporting Information?   53
- **4.4** How to Use Supporting Materials?   56
- **4.5** Final Questions   58

**Final Speech Topic**

Sustainable Development Goal 7: Affordable and Clean Energy   59

## Unit 5: Organizing Speeches   63

- **5.1** Why Is a Good Structure Important to a Speech?   65
- **5.2** How to Select the Main Ideas?   67
- **5.3** How to Organize the Main Ideas of a Speech?   68
- **5.4** How to Make Ideas Flow Nicely Using Language?   72
- **5.5** Final Questions   74

**Final Speech Topic**

Sustainable Development Goal 5: Gender Equality   74

## Unit 6: Beginning and Ending Speeches   77

- **6.1** Why Is an Introduction Important to a Speech?   79
- **6.2** How to Structure the Introduction of a Speech?   80
- **6.3** How to Get the Audience's Attention?   82
- **6.4** How to Structure the Conclusion of a Speech?   86
- **6.5** Final Questions   88

**Final Speech Topic**

Sustainable Development Goal 8: Decent Work and Economic Growth   89

## Unit 7 — Creating Speech Outlines — 93
- 7.1 What Is a Speech Outline? — 95
- 7.2 Why Do You Need an Outline? — 96
- 7.3 How to Create an Outline? — 97
- 7.4 Final Questions — 103

**Final Speech Topic**
Sustainable Development Goal 6: Clean Water and Sanitation — 104

## Unit 8 — Giving Informative Speeches — 107
- 8.1 What Is an Informative Speech? — 109
- 8.2 How to Design an Informative Speech? — 109
- 8.3 Final Questions — 116

**Final Speech Topic**
Sustainable Development Goal 1: No Poverty — 117

## Unit 9 — Giving Persuasive Speeches — 121
- 9.1 What Is a Persuasive Speech? — 123
- 9.2 Why Is It Difficult to Persuade People? — 123
- 9.3 How to Reduce the Constraints on Persuasive Speeches? — 124
- 9.4 How to Structure a Persuasive Speech? — 126
- 9.5 Exemplifying Structuring Persuasive Speeches: the Motivation Sequence — 128
- 9.6 Final Questions — 132

**Final Speech Topic**
Sustainable Development Goal 14: Life Below Water — 132

## Unit 10 — Performing Speeches — 137
- 10.1 How to Use Notes During Speaking? — 139
- 10.2 How to Use Voice to Make Your Presentation More Interesting? — 141
- 10.3 How to Use Your Body to Make Your Presentation More Interesting? — 144
- 10.4 How to Use Visuals to Make Your Presentation More Interesting? — 146
- 10.5 Final Questions — 148

**Final Speech Topic**
Sustainable Development Goal 17: Partnerships for the Goals — 148

## Appendix
Work Together to Build a Community of Shared Future for Mankind — 151

# Unit 1
# Introducing Public Speaking

# OBJECTIVES

After studying this unit, you should be able to:

(1) Understand what public speaking is in terms of the communication process.

(2) Describe a rhetorical situation and its three parts.

(3) Avoid plagiarism and learn to be an ethical speaker.

(4) Think positively and deal with your nervousness.

# Warm Up

## In Pairs

*1) Since you were small kids, you were told that wasting food is not appropriate. Why do you think wasting food is inappropriate? List out at least two reasons below and compare your answers with your partner.*

| Reason 1 |
|---|
| Reason 2 |

Unit 1   Introducing Public Speaking

*2) While your partner is speaking, do you think he or she has met the following criteria as a public speaker?*

|  | Yes | No |
|---|---|---|
| (1) Are the ideas presented clear enough that you can retell them? | ☐ | ☐ |
| (2) Did he or she look into your eyes during speaking so that you could feel being communicated? | ☐ | ☐ |
| (3) Could you feel the nervousness of your partner? | ☐ | ☐ |
| (4) Are you interested in finding out more about what he or she talked about? | ☐ | ☐ |

## 1.1   What Is Public Speaking?

Public speaking is communicating your messages to other people. To understand how this communication takes place in public, let's examine the communication process. As shown in the figure below, this process involves a message being encoded by the sender in a certain situation, and delivered through a channel to the receiver who then decodes the message (with the interference of the noise) and gives feedback to the sender. As you will see, treating your speech as communication in this way will help you make your message as clear as possible.

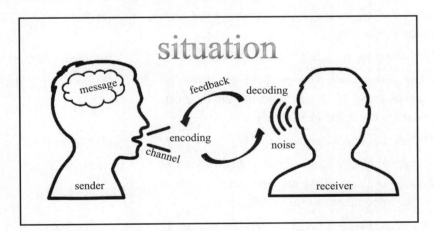

The following diagram shows a communication process and the eight elements involved.

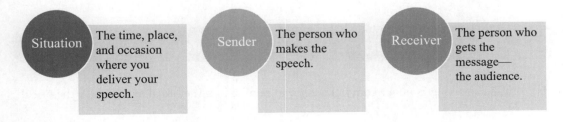

**Encoding** How the sender decides to send the message, including words used, visuals, formality, etc.

**Channel** How the message is delivered—verbal, visual or written; in person or online.

**Decoding** How the receiver understands the message based on his or her experiences.

**Noise** Things that can negatively affect the successful sending of the message. For example:
• problems in giving the speech, like a broken computer;
• opinions of the audience;
• a speech that is not clear.

**Feedback** The response of the receiver. For example:
• laughing, nodding, sleeping.

## Activity 1.1  Matching

*Read through the examples in Column A and match them to the elements in Column B. Draw a line between the items. Then compare your answers with your partner.*

**Column A**

(1) You have to give a speech on your project, in a classroom, at 2 pm.

(2) Delivering the speech in the form of Vlog.

(3) During the speech, some people listen carefully, some laugh out loud, and some take out their cell phones to check the messages.

(4) The speaker and the audience.

(5) The speaker says "An apple a day keeps the doctors away", and the audience understands it as "the importance of fruit in daily meal".

(6) The audience does not think you are an expert on this topic so they do not want to listen to you.

**Column B**

(a) Situation

(b) Sender & receiver

(c) Encoding & decoding

(d) Channel

(e) Noise

(f) Feedback

## 1.2  How Does "Being in Public" Affect Your Speaking?

Public speaking is about communicating in public, in a rhetorical situation. A rhetorical

# Unit 1　Introducing Public Speaking

situation means an occasion where you speak to a group of people. There are three parts in a rhetorical situation, namely the audience, the occasion and the speaker.

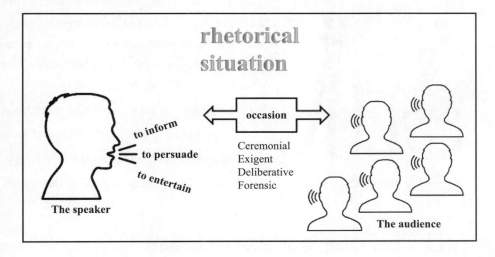

## 1. The Audience

The audience is the people listening to your speech. They can affect your speech in many ways, such as the language you use or the topic you choose. We will have a more detailed discussion about audience in Unit 2.

## 2. The Occasion

There are four types of occasions in public speaking. Each of them requires different speeches.

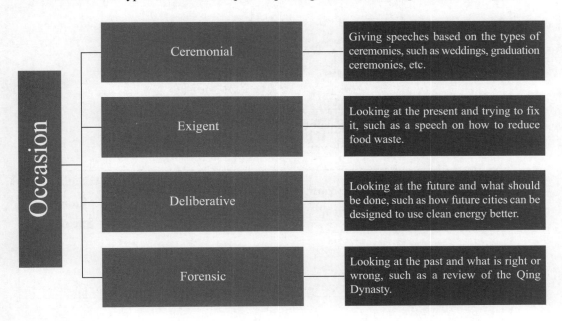

## 3. The Speaker

Each speaker is unique. Recall your performance in the Warm Up. You had different knowledge on the subject from your partner, a different opinion, and a different presentation style. In addition, different talks require different aims, such as:

(1) to inform: to tell the audience something;

(2) to persuade: to change the listeners' minds;

(3) to entertain: to make the audience happy.

Therefore, the uniqueness and the purpose of the speaker can greatly affect the speech.

## Activity 1.2    Analyzing Rhetorical Situations

### In Pairs

*Imagine a speech on the topic of "Food Safety". Look at the following rhetorical situations first. Then discuss with your partner the differences between them and complete the table below.*

| Rhetorical Situations | Who Are Your Audience? | What Is the Occasion? | Who Is the Speaker? | What Is the Aim of the Speaker? |
|---|---|---|---|---|
| A press conference after a food safety scandal | | | | |

Unit 1　Introducing Public Speaking

(Continued)

| Rhetorical Situations | Who Are Your Audience? | What Is the Occasion? | Who Is the Speaker? | What Is the Aim of the Speaker? |
|---|---|---|---|---|
| A dinner party celebrating the achievements of a politician improving food safety | | | | |
| A meeting of a food company trying to improve its image | | | | |

## 1.3　How to Be a Responsible Public Speaker?

### 1. Be Ethical.

Ethics means doing the right thing. A couple of other words that have a similar meaning include "morals" and "integrity".

Being ethical is important, because it shows:

(1) Respect to the listener.

- You want to give a speech that is worth the listener's time.

(2) Respect to the topic.

- The topic needs to be researched well so that you can speak like an expert.

(3) Respect to the occasion.

- Your speech needs to be suitable for the occasion otherwise people will react badly.

### 2. Avoid Plagiarism.

Plagiarism means copying work from somebody else and claiming it is your own.

Plagiarizing should be avoided for the reason that:

(1) It is stealing.

(2) It can hurt your reputation.

(3) It does not respect the audience, topic or occasion.

To avoid plagiarism, you can:

(1) Use quoting.

    • Quote exactly what another person has said, and refer to the orginal source.

(2) Use paraphrasing.

    • Re-tell in your own words what another person has said.

(3) Refer to the original source.

    • Refer to the original author, book, article, website, etc.

## Activity 1.3   Paraphrasing Ideas

### Step 1

### In Pairs

*Take a moment to observe the following images. Then discuss the following questions with your partner.*

(1) What do you see? Are you familiar with any of these images?

(2) What global issues are represented by these images? Choose one to discuss with your partner.

Unit 1  Introducing Public Speaking

## Step 2

## In Pairs

*1) The passage below gives some information about the United Nations Sustainable Development Goals (SDGs)[1]. These goals will form part of this textbook's content. Read the passage and identify THREE major ideas concerning SDGs, each idea per paragraph. Write them down in the box below. Then take turns paraphrasing what SDGs are about to each other.*

The Sustainable Development Goals are a universal call for action to end poverty, protect the planet and improve the lives and prospects of everyone, everywhere. The 17 goals were adopted by all UN Member States in 2015, as part of the 2030 Agenda for Sustainable Development. It set out a 15-year plan to achieve the goals.

Now, with less than 10 years left to achieve the Sustainable Development Goals, world leaders at the SDGs Summit in 2019 called for a Decade of Action. They recognized that ending poverty and other deprivations must go hand-in-hand with strategies that improve health, education, reduce inequality, and spur economic growth, meanwhile tackling climate change and working to preserve our oceans and forests.

The UN Secretary General called on all sectors of society to mobilize for a Decade of Action on three levels: global action to secure greater leadership, more resources and smarter solutions for the Sustainable Development Goals; local action including the needed transitions in the policies, budgets, institutions and regulatory frameworks of governments, cities and local authorities; and **people action**, including by youth, civil society, the media, the private sector and academia to generate an unstoppable movement pushing for the transformations.

| Paraphrasing Main Ideas of SDGs | |
|---|---|
| Idea 1 | |
| Idea 2 | |
| Idea 3 | |

*2) When paraphrasing, remember to include who said it (e.g. the United Nations) and where the information comes from (e.g. the United Nations Website). Use the following*

---

1 The United Nations. 2020. The Sustainable Development Agenda. *The United Nations*. Retrieved June 21, 2022, from The United Nations website.

*expressions when paraphrasing.*

| According to… | … said that… | It is mentioned by… |
| As… said, | As pointed out by… | It is suggested by… that… |

## 1.4 How to Speak More Confidently?

### 1. It Is Normal to Fear.

Never think yourself the only one who feels scared of being in front of people. I am scared. She is, and he is for sure. You will never be able to completely overcome fear. But you can feel your fear, and tell yourself "It's okay to fear".

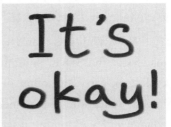

Also, some fear can actually be a good thing. A little bit of nervousness can really help you be more focused and excited when giving a speech.

### 2. How to Deal with Fear?

(1) Plan well.

- If you have researched the speech well, and have a logical structure, then it can be easier to be more confident.

(2) Visualize yourself giving the speech.

- It can help you get a clear picture in your mind of your speech, and you can see how you might look in front of the audience.

(3) Know that confidence comes with experience.

- The more you practice speaking in public, the more confident you would become.

(4) Change your outlook.

- Consider trying to see a speech not as a moment of fear, but as a challenge that you can overcome.

(5) Remember that the only person that knows the plan is yourself.

- If you change or miss a word during your speech, the only person that knows this is yourself. In fact, some of the best speeches are done by people who are flexible and are not afraid to change things in the middle of their speeches.

Unit 1　Introducing Public Speaking

## 1.5　Final Questions

(1) What is public speaking in terms of the communication process?

(2) What are the different parts of a rhetorical situation?

(3) What does "being ethical" mean and why is it important?

(4) How can you be more confident when speaking in public?

# Final Speech Topic

### The Rhetorical Situation

You are invited to talk at the Youth Forum held by the World Food Program, the world's largest humanitarian organization focusing on food assistance. Your task is to inform the audience of Sustainable Development Goal 12, and also introduce China's Clean Plate Campaign (its why, what and how) from your own perspective as a university student. Your aim of this speech is to make others know better about this campaign, and how the world can use a similar method to ensure food security.

### Step 1

*Read the report[1] about Sustainable Development Goal 12 "Responsible Consumption and Production", and discuss the following questions with your partner.*

(1) What is addressed in Goal 12?

(2) Why is this goal important?

(3) What are the problems identified in relation to this goal?

(4) What obstacles do members of your community face regarding waste of food?

---

1　The United Nations. 2020. Goal 12: Ensure sustainable consumption and production patterns. *The United Nations*. Retrieved June 21, 2022, from The United Nations website.

 **ENSURE SUSTAINABLE CONSUMPTION AND PRODUCTION PATTERNS**

## 1. What Is Goal 12?

It is to ensure sustainable food consumption and production patterns.

## 2. Why Is It Important? What Are the Problems?

Food loss is caused by the global material footprint; that is, food being transported from one location to another in order to satisfy our needs. Currently, we lose 13.8% after harvesting and during transport, storage, and processing. Also, by wasting food, we are polluting water faster than nature can recycle and purify it in rivers and lakes, not to mention the energy that is consumed to process the waste. The following table gives you a glimpse of the global situation of food waste, in the form of numbers.

| | **Annual Food Waste** | **Annual Carbon Footprint** | **Annual Water Waste** |
|---|---|---|---|
| **Data of Global Food Waste** | The annual amount of food waste globally reaches 1.6 billion tons, 1.3 billion tons of which are still edible. | The annual carbon footprint made by wasted food equates to 3.3 billion tons of greenhouse gases. | Global food production every year consumes 250 cubic kilometers water. |

## Step 2

*You are about to read China's solution in relation to Goal 12, in particular how China has focused on reducing food waste. Read the report[1] and discuss the following questions with your partner.*

(1) How has the "Clean Plate Campaign" changed over time? What has remained the same?

(2) How does reducing food waste contribute to sustainable development, at the social, economic and environmental levels?

---

1 Xian, J. N. 2020. China launches clean plate campaign 2.0 as Xi calls for end to food waste. *People's Daily Online*. Retrieved June 21, 2022, from People's Daily Online website.

# Unit 1　Introducing Public Speaking

## 3. What Is China's Solution?

China launched the "Clean Plate Campaign" in 2013. And in 2020, its 2.0 version arrived. Different from the previous campaign, which was aimed at putting an end to officials' extravagant feasts and receptions, the 2.0 version calls for the public to stop wasting food. The initiative initially sparked speculation by some media on whether China is in a food crisis. Experts say the world indeed faces a food shortage, but for China, the real threat to food security comes more from food wastage than epidemics or floods. With this 2.0 version, several goals are to be met:

(1) To make people aware of food waste, and maintain a sense of crisis of food security.

(2) To cultivate thrifty habits, and foster a social environment where waste is shameful and thriftiness is good.

(3) To reduce food waste and increase sustainability on the environment.

## Step 3

*With the notes from your reading and discussion, prepare a speech based on the rhetorical situation given in this unit. Do not forget to have a communicative awareness when designing your speech. Also, practice speaking in front of your classmates, as it is so far the best way to help build up your confidence.*

# Unit 2
# Analyzing the Audience

# OBJECTIVES

After studying this unit, you should be able to:

(1) Understand audience demographics and know how to use it for your speech.

(2) Observe cultural differences and know how to avoid stereotyping.

(3) Identify the audience's feelings about the topic, the occasion and yourself.

(4) Learn how to research about the audience.

# Warm Up

**Step 1**

In Groups

*In a group of four, discuss the following questions about environment to get an idea as to what your group members might believe.*

(1) What do you think are the major environmental issues in your community[1]?

---

1 As suggested by Britannica, there are three major pollutions on Earth: air, land and water pollution. Along with these, there are also plastic pollution, noise pollution, light pollution, and thermal pollution that are related closely to urban livings. More information on the causes and effects of these pollutions can be found at "Different Types of Pollution". *Britannica*. Retrieved June 22, 2022, from Britannica website.

# Unit 2  Analyzing the Audience

(2) What are causing these environmental problems?

(3) How can you fix these environmental problems?

## Step 2

## In Groups

*Now, consider the three questions above again, but this time from the point of view of your grandparents. Discuss the following questions within the group.*

(1) What differences can you see in the answers?

(2) Why do you think there are differences in viewpoints?

## 2.1  What Is Audience Demographics?

### 1. General Demographics of the Audience

The audience's demographics would include the following aspects, and each one can greatly affect your speech.

(1) Size of the audience.

- Larger groups of listeners will require a more formal speech.
- Smaller groups allow for a more conversational type of speech as you are able to interact with more people.

(2) Diversity of the audience.

- The homogeneous audience (many people are similar to each other) require you to make a speech suitable to one type of people.
- The heterogeneous audience (many people are different to each other) require you to make a speech that is suitable for many different kinds of people.

(3) Motivation of the audience.

- The voluntary audience want to be there and are already motivated.
- The captive audience have to be there, and may need to be motivated.

(4) Location of the audience.

- The real-site audience are in front of you in person. You can interact with them, and feel their emotions more, but you are restricted in what you can use on the site.

- The online audience are watching you on their electronic devices. You can use resources on the Internet, and reach a greater number of people, but you may not know who is in your audience. This makes it more difficult to get your real meaning across.

## Activity 2.1　Knowing Your Audience

In Pairs

*Imagine you were going to give a speech on "Me and My City" in front of your class about "How has your hometown reduced carbon emission in the last five years?" The following table provides a list of questions that will guide you through each aspect of the audience demographics. Work in pairs and analyze your audience by answering these questions.*

|  | **Audience Demographics Analysis** | **Your Answer** |
|---|---|---|
| **Size** | How many student-audience are there in your class? |  |
|  | How formal are you expected to be? |  |
| **Diversity** | Are your audience similar to one another? In what ways are they similar? |  |
|  | Are your audience different from one another? In what ways are they different? |  |

Unit 2   Analyzing the Audience

(Continued)

|  | Audience Demographics Analysis | Your Answer |
|---|---|---|
| **Motivation** | How much do your audience want to listen to you talking on the given subject? |  |
|  | What can you do to make your audience more interested in hearing you talking? |  |
| **Location** | Are you together with your audience in the same room? |  |
|  | How can you interact with your audience? |  |

Below is a list of more specific demographic information which would help you guide your audience analysis.

## 2. Specific Demographics of the Audience

Specific demographic information of the audience normally includes the following items:

(1) Gender.
- It can be dangerous to assume differences based on gender. Be careful here. More on this later when we discuss stereotyping.

(2) Age.

(3) Ethnicity.

(4) Education level.

(5) Economic status.

(6) Group membership.
- Do many people belong to a group that can influence their opinions on the topic?

**Note:** This list of audience specific demographics is not a complete list. There can be other ways you can analyze your audience.

## Activity 2.2   Collecting Demographic Information

## By Yourself

*Use your notes from Activity 2.1, and analyze your class for more specific demographics by filling in the table below. Interview one or two to help you with the table.*

|  | Homogeneous or Heterogeneous? | Opinions, Beliefs, and Ideas They Already Have? | How Would You Use This Information for Your Speech? |
|---|---|---|---|
| Gender | | | |
| Age | | | |
| Ethnicity | | | |
| Education Level | | | |
| Economic Status | | | |
| Group Membership | | | |
| Other _____ | | | |

## In Pairs

*Compare the answers to the above questions with your partner. Then discuss how you can use this information when creating your speech on the topic "Me and My City".*

## 2.2 What Are Audience Culture and Stereotyping?

As mentioned earlier, a group of audience can be defined either as homogeneous or heterogeneous, depending on whether or not the audience share the same set of beliefs, values, knowledge, interests and experience. When speaking to a group that are not similar to you, there is a danger of offending them. One of the easiest, and maybe the most dangerous ways to offend people, is through stereotyping.

Stereotyping is when you assume that all people in a group are the same, whereas in reality, they are very different from one another. Stereotyping can be dangerous because:

(1) It does not represent everybody in that group.

(2) It is very likely to be wrong and may offend your audience.

(3) It may be prejudicial and may offend your audience.

(4) It makes you appear narrow-minded.

Below are some hints for you to avoid stereotyping:

(1) Remember that people are unique.
- Don't try to make some cultural groups seem superior to other groups.

(2) Consider whether your ideas are based on facts or gossips.
- Do proper research. Don't use ideas that are not true.

(3) Don't assume everybody thinks the same as you.
- Embrace the differences and use them in your speech.

(4) Examine your motivations.
- Think about your audience. Don't try to make yourself seem superior.

## 2.3 What Do You Know About the Audience's Psychology, and How Can You Use It?

Understanding the psychology of the audience helps you understand why they are at your speech, what they choose to pay attention to, and how they interpret the messages of your speech. All of these details are important for you to remember when planning. There are three ways to categorize an audience's psychology:

### 1. Selective Exposure

People tend to choose to attend speeches for messages that they already agree with, or are important to them personally.
- If the audience is voluntary, then they may already agree with you and are trying to reinforce their own ideas.
- If the audience is captive, some people will agree with you, while others may not want to listen to you as your speech challenges their own beliefs, or is not of interest to them.

### 2. Selective Attention

People tend to take in information based on their own beliefs. They pay attention to what they consider important information and ignore the rest.

## 3. Perception

People tend to understand a message according to their own experiences. This can lead to a misunderstanding of the real message you are trying to give.

### Activity 2.3  Knowing Your Audience's Psychology

**Step 1**

## In Pairs

*Imagine a famous Chinese architect was giving a speech at your university, on how to make buildings more environmentally friendly. Discuss the following questions with your partner from the perspective of the audience.*

    (1) Would you choose to attend this speech? Why or why not?

    (2) If you were forced to attend this speech, would you pay attention? Why or why not?

    (3) What is your current opinion on making buildings environmentally friendly?

    (4) If the speaker says people should make all buildings environmentally friendly, what do you think you would do?

**Step 2**

## In Pairs

*How would you use your own psychological features as an audience to design your own speech "Me and My City"? Discuss in pairs and answer the questions below.*

    (1) How would you use "selective exposure" (voluntary or forced) to design your speech?

    (2) How would you use "selective attention" (you have your own beliefs on the topic) to design your speech?

    (3) How would you use "perception" (understanding comes from personal experience) to design your speech?

## 2.4  How to Find Out More About the Audience?

Before going to a speech, the audience may have some ideas already. These ideas can be about the topic, the occasion and you, the speaker. So it is important to explore and understand more about your audience so as to design a better speech that is audience-centered.

(1) How interested are they in the topic?

- Design a catchy introduction or a unique style for your speech, as the audience may have a low level of interest in the topic. It's your job to motivate them.

(2) What is their prior understanding of the topic?

- Consider what your audience know, and more importantly, don't know about your topic. You may need to give some background information first to help them understand your points.

(3) What do they think about the topic?

- They may have opinions already about this topic, and then you will need to know these so that you can change your speech accordingly.

(4) How do they feel about the occasion?

- Think about the speech occasion and the possible expectations the audience may have. Different occasions trigger different expectations on the content, style, and level of formality.

(5) How do they feel about you?

- You need to establish that you are worth listening to. If the audience have a negative opinion of you, then you need to win them over.

As shown below, there are many ways you can get more information about your audience. Therefore, choose the methods that are available to you and work best for you.

| Formal Methods | Informal Methods |
|---|---|
| **Market Research**<br>• Pay a business company to do the research for you.<br><br>**Audience Survey**<br>• Give the audience questionnaires to get the information you need. | • Use your past experience.<br>• Remember what people have told you before.<br>• Ask the person who gave you the speech some questions.<br>• Talk to people who are similar to your audience.<br>• Look online for research on your audience.<br>• Look at the materials your audience like. |

# Activity 2.4  Audience Survey

## Step 1

## By Yourself

*Complete the survey below by yourself. Go around and interview a couple of students. The related speech task is below this survey, as shown in "Final Speech Topic". Have a look to inform yourself about the speech topic and purposes.*

| Frequency of Using Shared Bikes | Age | Gender | Education Level |
|---|---|---|---|
| • Almost everyday | | | |
| • On a weekly basis | | | |
| • On a monthly basis | | | |
| • Seldom | | | |

| What Do You Think of the Following Statements? | Strongly Disagree | Slightly Disagree | Neither Agree nor Disagree | Slightly Agree | Strongly Agree |
|---|---|---|---|---|---|
| Riding a shared bike is more convenient than taking a public transit. | | | | | |
| Riding a shared bike is more environmentally friendly than taking a bus or driving a car. | | | | | |
| Riding a shared bike helps me save money. | | | | | |
| I get more exercise when riding a shared bike. | | | | | |

## Step 2

## In Groups

*Join your neighboring pair and form a group of four. Share the results of your survey within the group and discuss the following questions.*

(1) What common answers did you find?

Unit 2  Analyzing the Audience

(2) What differences did you see?

(3) How co uld you use this information in a speech about promoting green commuting?

## 2.5  Final Questions

(1) What are audience demographics, and what elements are included?

(2) How can you use the demographic information to plan your speech?

(3) What dangers may you face when speaking to people of different cultures?

(4) What may the audience feel about your speech, and how can you use this to design your speech?

# Final Speech Topic

### The Rhetorical Situation

*You are going to give a talk to your local community. Your goal is to make the audience become aware of Sustainable Development Goal 11 "Sustainable Cities and Communities". You decide to focus on shared bikes, and how they can contribute to Goal 11, by making cities greener, travel lighter and lives more sustainable.*

### Step 1

*Read the report[1] about Sustainable Development Goal 11 "Sustainable Cities and Communities", and discuss the following questions with your partner.*

(1) What is addressed in Goal 11?

(2) Why is this goal important?

---

1 The United Nations. 2020. Goal 11: Sustainable cities and communities. *The United Nations*. Retrieved June 21, 2022, from The United Nations website.

(3) What are the pressing problems for today's cities?

(4) How can shared bikes help to solve the problems mentioned above?

**MAKE CITIES AND HUMAN SETTLEMENTS INCLUSIVE, SAFE, RESILIENT AND SUSTAINABLE**

## 1. What Is Goal 11?

To make cities inclusive, safe, resilient and sustainable.

## 2. Why Is It Important?

The world is becoming increasingly urbanized. Over half of the world's population has lived in cities and this number continues to rise. It means that cities are facing worsening air pollution, inadequate infrastructure and services, and unplanned urban sprawl. Cities account for around 60% of global GDP, but they also account for more than 70% of global carbon emissions and 60% of resource use.

Many COVID-19 cases are occurring in urban areas. But on the other hand, there are also successful examples of containing COVID-19 in cities. This shows the remarkable resilience and adaptability of urban communities in adjusting to new norms.

## 3. What Are the Pressing Challenges Cities Face Today?

Major challenges include inequality, urban energy consumption, and pollution. Cities occupy just 3% of the Earth's land, but account for 60%–80% of energy consumption, and 75% of carbon emissions. Many cities are also more vulnerable to climate change and natural disasters because of their high concentration of people and buildings. It is therefore very crucial for cities to avoid human, social and economic losses. All these issues will eventually affect every one of us. Inequality may lead to unrest and insecurity; pollution affects our health and workers' productivity, and therefore economy; natural disasters may disrupt everyone's lifestyles.

Unit 2   Analyzing the Audience

## 4. How Can We Help by Riding a Shared Bike?[1]

Bike-sharing systems (BSSs) are a mobility service of public bikes that are available for shared use. This is becoming increasingly popular in cities. These shared systems give city residents an alternative, more sustainable and carbon-free mode of transportation, especially suited for short-distance trips. Comparing to taking a taxi or even a bus, riding a bike is always greener as it consumes no gas and so has zero carbon emission. So, the wide usage of shared bikes can significantly reduce traffic congestion, air pollution and noise pollution in cities, and also support the greener growth of urban environment.

### Step 2

*With the notes from your reading and discussion, prepare a speech based on the given rhetorical situation. Spend some time to learn more about your audience, and apply the information to plan your speech. You can also use your notes from Activity 2.1 to Activity 2.3 and the survey from Activity 2.4 when designing the speech.*

---

1 Caggiani, L. & Camporeale, R. 2021. Toward sustainability: Bike-sharing systems design, simulation and management. *MDPI Journal*. Retrieved June 24, 2022, from MDPI Journal website.

# Unit 3
# Designing Topics and Purposes

# OBJECTIVES

After studying this unit, you should be able to:

(1) Understand the importance of a speech with a good topic and clear purposes.

(2) Select appropriate and interesting topics.

(3) Make a topic more specific by narrowing it down.

(4) Specify the general purpose of a speech.

(5) Understand how the specific purpose and the thesis statement fit into the overall design of a speech.

# Warm Up

## In Pairs

*1) Your teacher is going to give each pair a topic from the list below. With your given topic, your pair will have one minute to write down two questions that can be used in a speech.*

Unit 3  Designing Topics and Purposes

*Once you finish, pass the piece of paper to the next pair, who will have one minute to write down two new questions. Continue this process until your teacher tells you to stop. Then collect your original piece of paper.*

   (1) Healthy food

   (2) Healthy activities

   (3) Healthy jobs

   (4) Healthy mind

   (5) Healthy medicine

*2) Once you have your original piece of paper back, have a look at all of the questions that were written. Which of the questions do you think can be used?*

   (1) To make an interesting speech to your classmates?

   (2) To make the speech more focused and specific?

   (3) To make an impact on the audience?

## 3.1  Why Do You Need a Topic and Purposes for Your Speech?

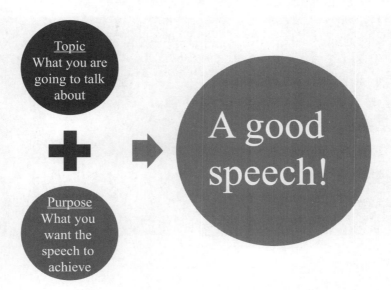

From the Warm Up activity, we can see that a speech with a good topic and clear purposes can:

## 1. Interest the audience.

The topic you've decided to choose should first of all be the one that you know a lot about, and at the same time, really excite your audience. Remember that the speech is for them, not for you.

## 2. Influence the audience.

A good topic can influence the audience to think in a way that you want them to. It has the aim of either to inform or to persuade, and it is worth spending time on.

## 3. Help focus on the speech.

When you have a good topic and a clear purpose, you know exactly what you want to achieve in the speech, and every decision you make when planning the speech will be affected by this focus.

### Activity 3.1  Analyzing a Given Topic

# Unit 3　Designing Topics and Purposes

## In Pairs

*Imagine you were asked to speak to your class on "The Importance of Good Health for Today's University Students". Use the guiding questions below to work out a good topic.*

(1) What are the three key words in the given topic?

(2) Can you choose one key word, and think of two completely different definitions for it?

(3) Is there anything missing from the topic that you can add to make it unique?

(4) Can you make this general topic more specific?

(5) Is there a way of making the topic more attractive to your audience?

## 3.2　How Can You Choose a Really Good Topic?

Very often, when you are given a speech to do, the topic may be given to you, as in Activity 3.1. In these moments, you do not have much freedom. However, you might be surprised about how much creativity you can have. The questions above have helped you find new perspectives on a given topic:

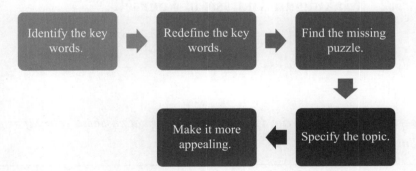

There can be other times when you are given a very general topic, or not even a topic at all. It can be challenging to be creative at these times. Here are some tips to guide you when you don't know where to start:

## 1. Analyzing Yourself.

It is important to know what you are really enthusiastic about, something that you would love to tell your friends. Your audience can also feel your passion about the topic, and so become interested in hearing more.

Equally important, you need to know what you are good at. It would make your speech a lot easier if you choose something you know a lot about, or you are most familiar with. Hopefully, you can find some similarities in these with your audience.

### Activity 3.2    Making an Analysis of Yourself

**Step 1**

### By Yourself

*Create a personal inventory. Write down as much information about yourself as possible in the following categories.*

| Personal Inventory |
| --- |
| Name |
| Hometown |
| Educational background |
| Academic interests |

Unit 3  Designing Topics and Purposes

(Continued)

| Personal Inventory |
| --- |
| Hobbies |
| Special skills |
| Personal experiences |
| Favorite thing (or person, animal, etc.) |
| Concerns or beliefs (e.g. Internet privacy, family education, etc.) |

## Step 2

# By Yourself

*Now, think about the following questions based on the topic "The Importance of Good Health for Today's University Students".*

    (1) How much do you know about the topic?

    (2) What part of the topic interests you most?

    (3) What is your opinion of the topic?

    (4) Where can you research more about the topic?

## Step 3

# In Pairs

*Share your personal inventory with your partner and look for common answers. What information can you find from your partner that can help you plan your own speech?*

                                                    Note Box

## 2. Analyzing Your Audience.

It is always the audience who decide whether your topic is good or boring. So, a cool topic is usually audience-centered, which has already been discussed in Unit 2. To analyze the audience, you should get to know who they are, what their interests are, and what they need to know.

## 3. Analyzing the Rhetorical Situation.

A good topic is one that considers carefully the rhetorical situation, which has been discussed in Unit 1. It means that the circumstance in which a person employs rhetoric to inform or persuade. For a good topic, you need to analyze the following two things in relation to the rhetorical situation:

- The occasion: Is your speech for a class, a seminar, a conference, or a financial report? There are so many occasions, and you need to find the right topic for the right occasion.
- The physical setting: Where does your speech take place? Imagine a speech on improving the environment at a conference, compared to a similar speech in a national park. The latter is definitely more convincing in regard to the topic and the physical context.

## 4. Analyzing Public Events.

When choosing your topic, think about recent events that are relevant to your topic. They can be events happening in your community, within the country, or around the world, something your audience might be aware of and following.

Channels such as newsreel, general interest websites, social media, can be helpful for you to see what is going on in regard to the topic. This can allow you to be more "in" with your topic, rather than relying on the same, "out" dated stories that someone has already used.

# Activity 3.3  Knowing More About Your Topic

## In Pairs

*Discuss the following questions with your partner.*

(1) What interests your classmates on the topic of "health and well-being"?

(2) If you were giving a speech to the fellow students at your university:

   a. What would be the occasion?

   b. Where would this speech take place?

Unit 3  Designing Topics and Purposes

c. What are some recent events at your university that are related to "health and well-being"?

(3) Have a look at a news website for any news on recent events that you can use (you might find some information in the science and health sections of the news).

(4) How would the answers to the above questions affect you when designing a topic "The Importance of Good Health for Today's University Students"? Write down your answers in the box below.

**Note Box**

5. Brainstorming for Ideas.

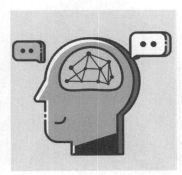

Some brainstorming techniques include:

**Starbursting**
- Write down all information and look for who, what, where, when, why and how.
- Consider how each of them can give you ideas on improving your topic.

**SWOT analysis**
- Look at the strengths, weaknesses, opportunities, and threats of the topic.
- Use your analysis to narrow down your topic.

| Mind mapping | • Put ideas on paper, with the key word in the center, and write down anything you can think of.<br>• It helps you quickly capture your thoughts, and form a structure for the speech. |

## Activity 3.4  Starbursting

### Step 1

### By Yourself

*Look at the Starbursting on the topic "Healthy Lives and Well-being" on the next page. Read through the example questions and think of some questions of your own. Write them down in the Starbursting Question Box below.*

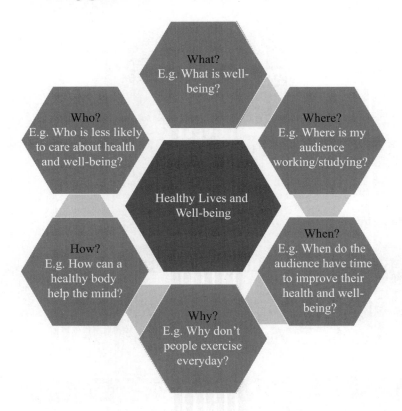

Unit 3　Designing Topics and Purposes

| Starbursting Question Box | |
|---|---|
| What | |
| Where | |
| When | |
| Why | |
| How | |
| Who | |

**Step 2**

## In Pairs

***Share your notes with your partner and discuss the following question.***

Which questions do you think would be useful and interesting for a speech to your classmates?

**Note Box**

## 3.3　How to Narrow Down a Topic?

Narrowing down the topic means to reduce how much you talk about, basically being more specific. It not only makes the speech more impressive, but also helps you control your materials as well. The result of this process is for you to know exactly what you are going to present within a limited time.

In general, for the audience who do not know much about a topic, you need to be general. For the audience who do know a lot about a topic, you need to be more specific. At university, the narrower the topic, the better! One way to narrow down a topic is by continually breaking the topic down into categories, until you are satisfied with the result.

# Activity 3.5　Breaking Down a Topic

## In Pairs

*Complete the figure below with the most general topic "Health" at the first level, and then narrow it down to a more specific level. Feel free to take it down a few more levels if you can.*

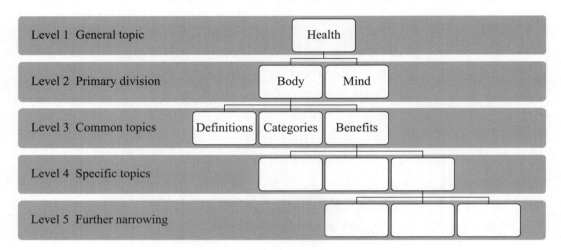

# 3.4　General Purpose, Specific Purpose & Thesis Statement

## 1. What Is a Purpose?

In every speech, the speaker is attempting to achieve something. What the speaker is attempting to do is called a "purpose". In public speaking, there can be a "general" purpose and a "specific" purpose.

## 2. What Is a General Purpose?

A general purpose is what you are trying to achieve overall. There are seven general purposes. So when preparing your speech, you need to choose from the list the one or ones you are going to try and achieve. The seven general purposes are:

(1) To make people feel good or bad about something.

(2) To make people start talking about something.

# Unit 3  Designing Topics and Purposes

(3) To give new information.

(4) To change people's opinion completely.

(5) To make people feel weaker about something.

(6) To make people feel stronger about something.

(7) To make people do something.

For example, in your speech about weight lifting as an exercise, you might want to:

- Give new information—explain why weight lifting is better for your heart than cardio, and/or

- Make people do something—get them to buy a pair of dumb bells for their stay-at-home training session.

The above two purposes, when combined, can be easily found in today's advertisements. So, the general purpose is a very useful tool in giving you choices—there are many different ways you can use to approach your speech.

## 3. What Is a Specific Purpose?

A specific purpose involves changing the general purpose to match the "specific" speech. The specific purpose helps you bring your idea into sharp focus and thus form a thesis statement and then the structure of the speech.

For example, the diagram below shows a speech topic "Health Care", and its general purposes "to give new information" and "to make people start talking". So one of the specific purposes could be "You want the audience to know about the five problems all countries must tackle now to achieve the 2030 health-related goals."

**Note:** This specific purpose includes the topic and the general purpose.

| Topic | General Purposes |
|---|---|
| • Health Care | • To give new information<br>• To make people start talking |

**Specific Purposes**

- To tell your audience that there are five health problems all countries need to tackle to achieve the SDG on health

- To make your audience become aware that if they don't do this, then it can be a problem for future generations

41

## 4. What Is a Thesis Statement?

A thesis statement is one sentence that can summarize your entire speech. It is the central idea, and states the claim made by your speech. The thesis statement can also be used directly in your introduction (see Unit 6 for how to make an introduction).

### Activity 3.6   Identifying

**In Pairs**

*The following article is a part of a speech which talks about a mosquito-transferred virus named "Zika". Read the article by yourself, and write down the general purpose, specific purpose and thesis statement in the box below. Then compare your answers with your partner.*

> ### A Secret Weapon Against Zika and Other Mosquito-borne Diseases[1]
>
>
>
> Zika fever, our newest dread disease. What is it? Where did it come from? What do we know about it? Well, for most adults, it's a relatively mild disease—a little fever, a little headache, joint pain, maybe a rash. In fact, most people who get it don't even know they've had it.
>
> But, the more we find out about the Zika virus, the more terrifying it becomes. For example, doctors have noticed an uptick of something called Guillain-Barré syndrome in recent outbreaks. In Guillain-Barré, your immune system attacks your nerve cells. It can partially or even totally paralyze you. Fortunately, that's quite rare, and most people recover. But, if you're pregnant when you're infected, you're at risk of something terrible.

---

1 Fedoroff, N. 2017. A secret weapon against Zika and other mosquito-borne diseases. *TEDx*. Retrieved March 19, 2022, from TEDx website.

Unit 3   Designing Topics and Purposes

(Continued)

> So, where did it come from? And how did it get here? It came out of Africa, specifically the Zika forest in Uganda. Researchers at the nearby Yellow Fever Research Institute identified an unknown virus in a monkey in the Zika forest, which is how it got its name.
>
> The first human cases of Zika fever surfaced a few years later in Uganda-Tanzania. The virus, then, spread through West Africa and east, through equatorial Asia—Pakistan, India, Malaysia, Indonesia. But, it was still mostly in monkeys and, of course, mosquitoes. In fact, in the 60 years between the time it was first identified in 1947, and 2007, there were only 13 reported cases of human Zika fever.
>
> And then, something extraordinary happened on the tiny Micronesian Yap islands. There was an outbreak that affected fully 75 percent of the population. How did it get there? By air. Today we have two billion commercial airline passengers. An infected passenger can board a plane, and fly halfway around the world before developing symptoms. Then when he/she land, the local mosquitoes begin to bite him/her and spread the fever.

(1) General purpose: _____
(2) Specific purpose: _____
(3) Thesis statement: _____

## 3.5   Final Questions

(1) Why do you need a good topic?

(2) How can you choose a good topic?

(3) How can you narrow down a topic?

(4) What are the seven general purposes?

(5) What is a thesis statement?

# Final Speech Topic

## The Rhetorical Situation

*With the ongoing COVID-19 pandemic and new mutations being regular occurrences, you have been asked to give a speech to the World Youth Scientist Summit to introduce China's ways to optimize the use of medical resources and meanwhile manage the spreading of the virus in public.*

### Step 1

*Read the report[1] about Sustainable Development Goal 3 "Good Health and Well-being", and discuss the following questions with your partner.*

(1) What is addressed in Goal 3?

(2) Why is this goal important?

(3) What are the problems identified in this goal?

**ENSURE HEALTHY LIVES AND PROMOTE WELL-BEING FOR ALL AT ALL AGES**

### 1. What Is Goal 3?

To ensure healthy lives and promote well-being for all at all ages.

### 2. Why Is It Important? What Are the Problems Behind This Goal?

Ensuring healthy lives and promoting well-being are important for building prosperous societies. However, the COVID-19 pandemic has devastated health systems globally and threatens already achieved health outcomes. Now, to achieve universal health coverage and sustainable financing for health, the biggest issues are insufficient health facilities, insufficient

---

1 The United Nations. 2020. Goal 3: Good health and well-being. *The United Nations*. Retrieved March 26, 2022, from The United Nations website.

Unit 3   Designing Topics and Purposes

medical supplies and insufficient health care workers.

## Step 2

*You are about to read a news report[1] introducing some of the methods China has adopted to tackle the Omicron variant. Read it through and discuss the following questions with your partner.*

    (1) What does China plan to do in tackling the insufficiency of medical resources due to the pandemic?

    (2) How can these methods help to meet Goal 3 and ensure healthy lives of all people?

## 3. What Does China Plan to Do for Universal Coverage of Health During the Pandemic?

    To solve the problem of lacking medical facilities, the country began to build facilities to reduce the burden on hospitals. These buildings are makeshift hospitals. Makeshift hospitals refer to facilities that are equipped with essential infrastructure such as water and electricity, toilets, shower rooms, ventilation systems as well as medical and protective equipment. The main purpose of makeshift hospitals is to take in mild and asymptomatic COVID-19 cases, so as to cut off the virus' transmission and also prevent overburdening regular hospitals.

    Because new infections will likely spike swiftly during an Omicron outbreak, makeshift hospitals are vital to accommodating cases and relieving the strain on regular healthcare services. In addition, makeshift hospitals can play a significant role in tackling other contagious diseases or other large-scale health emergencies. Such sites can begin receiving patients within 24 hours after a new outbreak is detected. Setting up more makeshift hospitals is not a sign of worsening epidemic conditions. Rather, it is to adapt to the traits of Omicron such as that it is highly contagious, spreads very quickly and the majority of infections are mild or asymptomatic.

## Step 3

*With the notes from your reading and discussion, prepare a speech based on the rhetorical situation given in this unit. Use what you have learnt in this unit, and spend some time choosing a good topic and clear purposes for your speech.*

---

1 Wang, X. 2022. Officials urged to plan ahead for Omicron. *China Daily*. Retrieved June 11, 2022, from China Daily website.

# Unit 4
# Using Supporting Information

# OBJECTIVES

After studying this unit, you should be able to:

(1) Understand what supporting information is and why it is important to a speech.

(2) Identify and describe seven types of supporting information.

(3) Locate and find your supporting information.

(4) Use your supporting information appropriately.

# Warm Up

**Step 1**

In Pairs

*Use the following questions to interview each other about personal opinions and experiences with clean energy. Each person takes about two minutes to speak. Remember to make notes about what the other person talks about.*

(1) What does clean energy mean to you?

(2) What are some examples of clean energy?

(3) Is clean energy important to you? Why or why not?

Unit 4　Using Supporting Information

```
┌─────────────────────────────────────────────┐
│                  Note Box                    │
│                                              │
│                                              │
│                                              │
│                                              │
└─────────────────────────────────────────────┘
```

**Step 2**

## In Groups

*Now, join another group of two people. Report to the other group what you learnt about your partner who you have just interviewed. When you report, quote what your partner has talked about. The following are examples to start your report.*

(1) My partner thinks that clean energy is… As he/she said…

(2) My partner talked about his/her understanding of clean energy. According to him/her, it means…

(3) Clean energy is very important. As mentioned by my partner…

## 4.1　What Is Supporting Information and Why Is It Important?

While quoting what your partner has said to back up his/her opinion on clean energy, you have successfully used what is called "supporting information". Supporting information is the evidence that you use to support an idea and to show what you are saying is correct. You can get supporting information by researching such as looking in books, academic journals, reputable Internet sites, and talking to people (as what was done in Warm Up).

Supporting information is particularly important in formal communications such as academic writings and business presentations because:

### 1. It Makes Your Argument Stronger.

Supporting information is evidence. Without this evidence, there is no proof that what is being said is actually true. People can make any claim they want. Therefore, by including credible supporting information, you are increasing the chances that people will agree with your points, and so increasing the chances that you will be successful in fulfilling the purpose of your speech.

## 2. It Helps You Know More About the Topic.

Researching on supporting information often leads to you finding out things that you may not have known before. This allows you to increase your knowledge on the topic, which you can then use in the speech. Also, there is a question time in some speeches once they are finished. The more you know about the topic, the better you can answer these questions.

## 3. It Helps You Make Your Speech More Interesting.

Searching for data, examples or stories can help you find some really interesting information that can make your speech more suitable and interesting for the audience.

## Activity 4.1

## In Pairs

*1) A speaker talks about the promotion of hydropower in his hometown. Read the sample speech and answer the questions below. Then summarize the speech to your partner with the help of your answer notes.*

> **Clean Energy in My Hometown**
>
> (1) The Ertan Dam was built on the Yalong River in Sichuan Province, and was opened in 1999. (2) According to reports by *Sichuan Online* in 2018, before the Dam was built, local residents had suffered from insufficient electricity for decades. (3) The power lines were often cut down to limit electricity consumption.
>
> (4) However, thanks to the Dam, the development in southwest China has been fully guaranteed. (5) For example, the steel industry in my hometown Panzhihua is empowered by the Ertan Dam to a large extent. (6) Panzhihua is a city near the Ertan Dam, and is one of China's largest producers of steel. (7) Imagine, without the Ertan Dam, many of the steel workers could lose their jobs. (8) Also, owing to the clean and sustainable hydropower, we have cut down coal consumption and reduced the $CO_2$ emission. (9) No wonder there is a saying that goes around in the area—"The Ertan Dam means a lot to Panzhihua."

Unit 4　Using Supporting Information

(1) What is the main idea of this speech? Underline the parts you think as the thesis statement and summarize them with one sentence.

(2) What supporting information is used to back up the main idea? Underline the parts you think as supporting information, and write the sentence numbers down below.

2) *What would happen if you erase all the supporting information you have underlined, leaving only the main idea? Give it a try and discuss the supporting information with your partner.*

## 4.2　What Kinds of Supporting Information Are There?

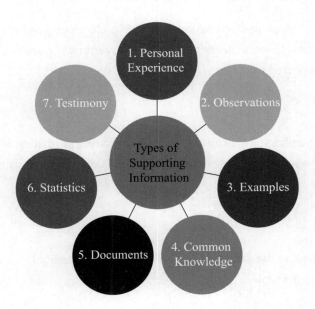

### 1. Personal Experience

Personal experience provides evidence based on things you have seen and experienced. This experience can make your speech "personal", and also add credibility.

### 2. Observations

While personal experience is something that happened naturally to you, an observation is more scientific. It would include a report and also an analysis of what you have seen. For example, you observe how a two-children family spend their weekends for a period of time.

## 3. Examples

Examples represent what you are trying to say, and are very common. Examples can be real or hypothetical case studies, and can also be long or short.

## 4. Common Knowledge

Common knowledge refers to things that most people know. We often use "As we all know" to indicate the use of common knowledge, but it is often inappropriate for academic speeches.

## 5. Documents

Documents are things that are written, printed or electronic, and act as official records. They can include newspapers, academic papers, government documents and many other records that are considered trustworthy.

## 6. Statistics

Statistics are numbers. This can be a great source of information if the statistics come from a trustworthy source and are used in an appropriate way. The misuse of statistics may harm credibility.

## 7. Testimony

Testimony means to use information given by another person. A testimony does need to be from an expert on the topic.

## Activity 4.2

### In Pairs

*Read through the examples in Column A and match them to the types in Column B. Draw a line between the items. Then compare your answers with your partner.*

Unit 4  Using Supporting Information

**Column A**

(1) 70% of students in this classroom believe that we should use renewable energy.

(2) The National Energy Administration has issued new guidelines on new energy projects.

(3) Your answers in the Warm Up activity.

(4) My mom told me that the wind turbines near my house were built when I was two years old.

(5) Energy is needed to power our phones.

(6) In Australia, the use of e-bikes is not common because the distances between spots are too long.

(7) Yesterday, I went to the local shopping center and watched how many people entered between the times of 6:00 pm and 7:00 pm.

**Column B**

(a) Personal experience

(b) Observations

(c) Examples

(d) Common knowledge

(e) Documents

(f) Statistics

(g) Testimony

## 4.3  Where to Find Supporting Information?

A list of common channels to look for your supporting materials include:

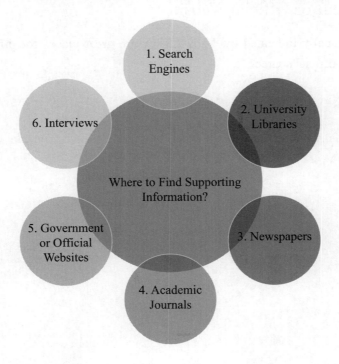

## 1. Search Engines

A search engine is a website that helps you find information. Common search engines include Baidu and Bing (International).

## 2. University Libraries

Libraries are good places for books and journal articles. However, libraries can be far away, or busy, or the book might not be there because somebody else has it. In these cases, you might be able to find resources through online libraries.

## 3. Newspapers

The biggest advantage of newspapers (including online newspapers) is that they have the most recent information. However, it is important to check the credibility of newspapers. Some newspapers are more trustworthy than others.

## 4. Academic Journals

Journal articles are written by people doing research on a topic, often university professors. You can read the introduction and conclusion of a journal article first, to get the key information and then decide if you need to read any more.

## 5. Government or Official Websites

These are usually indicated by ".gov". They are great places for information as the government is an official source.

## 6. Interviews

This is normally concerned with an expert talking on a topic. You can also do your own interview. But be aware to be on the topic and professional.

Unit 4  Using Supporting Information

# Activity 4.3

### Step 1

### By Yourself

*Read the sample speech below and identify the types of supporting information that you think have been used. Write down the sentence number according to the type of supporting information used.*

> **Clean Energy in My Hometown**
>
> (1) The Ertan Dam was built on the Yalong River in Sichuan Province, and was opened in 1999. (2) According to reports by *Sichuan Online* in 2018, before the Dam was built, local residents had suffered from insufficient electricity for decades. (3) The power lines were often cut down to limit electricity consumption.
>
> (4) However, thanks to the Dam, the development in south-west China has been fully guaranteed. (5) For example, the steel industry in my hometown Panzhihua is empowered by the Ertan Dam to a large extent. (6) Panzhihua is a city near the Ertan Dam, and is one of China's largest producers of steel. (7) Imagine, without the Ertan Dam, many of the steel workers could lose their jobs. (8) Also, owing to the clean and sustainable hydropower, we have cut down coal consumption and reduced the $CO_2$ emission. (9) No wonder there is a saying that goes around in the area—"The Ertan Dam means a lot to Panzhihua."

(1) Personal experience _____
(2) Observations _____
(3) Examples _____
(4) Common knowledge _____
(5) Documents _____
(6) Statistics _____
(7) Testimony _____

### Step 2

### In Pairs

*Now, compare your answers above with your partner. If there is a difference, explain and justify your answers and try to understand the difference. You can both be right.*

## Step 3

## In Pairs

*Look back at Step 1. Which types of supporting information were not used? How can you use the remaining types of supporting information in the speech about the Ertan Dam? Where can you find the information? Write down your answers below and discuss with your partner.*

**Note Box**

## 4.4 How to Use Supporting Materials?

After having collected your materials, you need to consider the most important issue—plagiarism. It means not using the materials as if they were your own. You need to give credit to the original producers of the materials you have in hand by referencing. There are two ways how you can use the materials while respecting the original authors.

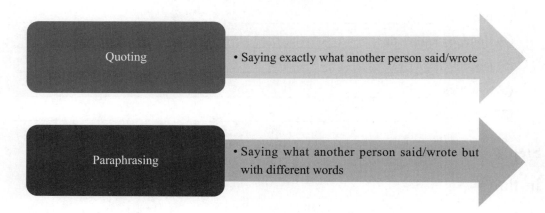

# Unit 4  Using Supporting Information

What is a reference? A reference provides the listeners with the source of the information. It includes:

- what they said or wrote;
- who said or wrote it;
- where you found it.

When quoting or paraphrasing information, you should give a reference. This is particularly true in academic work. If the source of information is credible, giving the reference makes your speech stronger. In fact, having lots of different references shows that you have done lots of research and it is a very good thing.

## Activity 4.4

### Step 1

### By Yourself

*Have a look at the supporting information that you found in Activity 4.3. Choose one piece of supporting information that you think is the strongest, and create a plan for how to use it below.*

(1) What type of supporting information is it?

(2) What is the quote?

(3) Who said/wrote it?

(4) Where did you find it?

(5) Why is the supporting information useful?

### Step 2

### By Yourself

*Write a paragraph using the supporting information you have chosen from Step 1. The following aspects should be paid attention to.*

(1) Write a topic sentence—a sentence that makes a claim.

(2) Quote or paraphrase the supporting information.

(3) Make the reference clear (who stated it, what was stated, and where you got it).

(4) Make the paragraph flow nicely.

**Your Paragraph**

## Step 3

## In Pairs

*Take turns reading the paragraph to each other. While listening to your partner, make some notes based on the following questions.*

(1) Was your partner's paragraph easy to understand?

(2) Was the supporting information referenced well?

(3) Was the supporting information appropriate for you?

(4) What improvements can you suggest?

**Note Box**

## 4.5　Final Questions

(1) What is supporting information?

(2) Why is supporting information important?

(3) What kinds of supporting information are there?

(4) How can you find your supporting information?

(5) How can you use the supporting information without getting caught plagiarizing?

Unit 4　Using Supporting Information

# Final Speech Topic

> ## The Rhetorical Situation
>
> *You are to talk about Sustainable Development Goal 7 "Affordable and Clean Energy" at a public event organized by your university's Environment Society. Your goal is to make students become aware of the goal, and the issues behind it. You should also encourage the audience to become more engaged in achieving Goal 7.*

## Step 1

*Read the report[1] about Sustainable Development Goal 7 "Affordable and Clean Energy", and discuss the following questions with your partner.*

    (1) What is Goal 7?

    (2) Why is this goal important?

    (3) What are the problems identified in this goal?

    (4) What can be done in order to solve the problems?

 **ENSURE ACCESS TO AFFORDABLE, RELIABLE, SUSTAINABLE AND MODERN ENERGY FOR ALL**

## 1. What Is Goal 7?

    Goal 7 is to ensure access to affordable, reliable, sustainable and modern energy for all. Modern energy is energy that does not rely on the traditional source of fossil fuels; instead it uses sources such as wind power, solar, hydropower and geothermal power.

---

1　The United Nations. 2020. Goal 7: Affordable and clean energy. *The United Nations*. Retrieved May 15, 2022, from The United Nations website.

## 2. Why Is It Important? What Are the Problems Behind This Goal?

There are still millions of people worldwide who don't have electricity. Just sub-Saharan Africa alone has a number of 548 million people without electricity service. With no electricity, women and girls have to spend hours fetching water, clinics cannot store vaccines and people cannot run good business. Not to mention the exposure to harmful household air pollution from cooking, mostly among women and children.

Also, for many decades, fossil fuels such as coal, oil and gas have been major sources of electricity production, but burning carbon fuels produces large amounts of greenhouse gases which cause climate change and have harmful impacts on people's health and the environment.

Clean, renewable energy provides a variety of environmental and economic benefits, including a reduction in air pollution. It also brings cost savings, as there is no need to extract and transport fuels and as the resources replenish themselves naturally. Also, it reduces the risk of environmental disasters such as fuel spills or natural gas leaks.

## 3. What Can Be Done?

Countries should speed up the change from using coal or fossil fuel, to the use of an affordable, reliable, and sustainable energy system. To make this transition process quicker, countries should increase the investment in renewable energy resources, prioritizing energy efficient practices, and adopting clean energy technologies and infrastructure.

Businesses can maintain and protect ecosystems such as grassland, desert, fresh water, ocean and so on, and can commit to sourcing 100 percent of operational electricity needs from renewable sources.

Employers can reduce the internal demand for transport by prioritizing telecommunications and incentivize less energy intensive modes such as train travel over auto and air travel.

# Unit 4  Using Supporting Information

Investors can invest more in sustainable energy services, bringing new technologies to the market quickly from a diverse supplier base.

You can save energy by plugging appliances into a power strip and turning them off completely when they are not in use, including your computer. You can also bike, walk or take public transport to reduce carbon emissions.

## Step 2

*With the notes from your reading and discussion, prepare a speech based on the rhetorical situation given in this unit. Use what you have learnt in this unit, and spend some time in selecting your supporting information. Also, consider how to use it appropriately in the speech.*

# Unit 5

## Organizing Speeches

# OBJECTIVES

After studying this unit, you should be able to:

(1) Understand why a good structure is important to your speech.

(2) Select the main ideas.

(3) Design the body of your speech.

(4) Make your ideas flow nicely through the use of language.

# Warm Up

# Unit 5　Organizing Speeches

## In Pairs

***Discuss the following questions with your partner. You can use the structure below to talk about your ideas.***

(1) What do you think gender empowerment is?

(2) Why do you think we may need to encourage gender empowerment?

(3) Can you think of any examples of gender empowerment?

> **Structure**
> - Define gender empowerment.
> - State why it is needed.
> - Discuss examples.

**Note:** A definition of "empowerment" can be found at the end of this unit. But you are encouraged to think on your own before looking at it.

## 5.1　Why Is a Good Structure Important to a Speech?

The structure of a speech is important for the following reasons:

### 1. It Helps the Audience Remember Your Points.

If you organize your ideas in a structural and logical way, it would be easier for the audience to remember this, and therefore remember your arguments. In the Warm Up, you have used a structure that can help your audience understand better your main point, i.e. your own understanding of gender empowerment.

### 2. It Helps the Audience Build a Relationship Between Ideas.

A well-structured body can help the audience make a link between ideas. The audience can see how one part relates to another. In the Warm Up, the structure of your presentation shows a link between your main idea and the examples you use to support it.

### 3. It Helps the Audience Anticipate What Will Happen Next.

A well-structured body can help the audience anticipate what will happen next. This can help them follow the structure better. And they feel a sense of achievement if they are correct in their guess.

## 4. It Helps the Speaker Check for Missing Information.

Having a nice structure can also help you, the speaker. If you have a logical organization of the body, you can possibly see if you are missing something.

## Activity 5.1　Identifying Main Ideas

*Below is part of a speech by Inese Podgaiska, the Secretary General of the Association of Nordic Engineers. She talked about gender digital empowerment in Europe. According to Makinen, digital empowerment refers to a person's perceived capacity to use digital technologies and his/her view of his/her competency in the digital world[1].*

## By Yourself

*Read the sample speech[2] and write down your answers to the questions below. Then compare your answers with your partner.*

---

**Digital Empowerment of Women**

Empowering women is a precondition for our economic growth, political stability and social transformation. In the modern world, female participation in the digital economy and society becomes particularly crucial. However, in Europe, half of the population cannot fully participate in their societies' digital development and life. Today, in my speech, I want to draw your attention to three specific barriers I experienced and observed during my professional life that interfere digital empowerment of women.

The first barrier is the lack of interest and stereotypes. We must have more girls and women interested in STEM subjects. To cultivate this interest, we must also break down the stereotypes, and encourage girls to study according to what they want to rather than what they can do. The second barrier is the lack of self-confidence. Most of the girls and women do not think they have the aptitude for solving maths and technical problems. The third barrier is the lack of equal opportunities. This means that often women are not enjoying the same privileges and opportunities.

---

1　Makinen, M. 2006. Digital empowerment as a process for enhancing citizens' participation. *SAGE Journal*. Retrieved July 5, 2022, from SAGE Journal website.

2　Podgaiska, I. Digital women empowerment. *Association of Nordic Engineers (ANE)*. Retrieved May 2, 2022, from Association of Nordic Engineers (ANE) website.

(1) What is the thesis statement of this speech?

(2) What are the main ideas used to talk about the thesis statement?

(3) Is there a link between the main ideas in this speech?

(4) What do you think are the general and specific purposes of this speech?

(5) Can the main ideas help achieve these purposes?

## 5.2 How to Select the Main Ideas?

In organizing the body of your speech, the first thing to do is choose your main ideas. Then you may wonder:

- What is a main idea? How can you choose it?

**Main ideas are the "claims" you are using to address the thesis statement.**

- How to select and structure the main ideas of a speech?

Here is a list of questions which would guide you in selecting and structuring.

### 1. Are Your Main Ideas Dependent on Each Other?

Do you need to go in a specific order to understand the speech? If yes, that speech would need to go in a special order.

### 2. Are Some Ideas More Familiar to the Audience than Other Ones?

It can be better to start with ideas that the audience know about, so that you can make them feel comfortable. You can use unfamiliar information later.

### 3. Should You Start with Strong or Weak Ideas?

The research on this has not proven which way is better, so you might need to think about your speech and audience first in deciding what to do.

## 5.3 How to Organize the Main Ideas of a Speech?

There are at least seven ways to organize the main ideas.

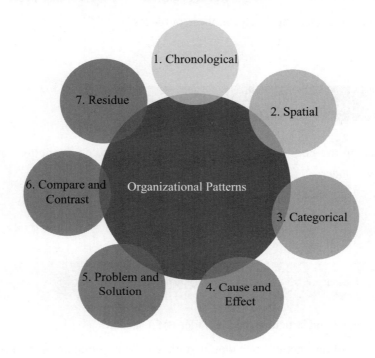

## 1. Chronological

This refers to the sequence of time, for example "Three years ago… And now… In the future…".

## 2. Spatial

This is related to space. Spatial organization means to organize the main ideas in a speech based on the place or position, and can include going from small to big, left to right, up to down or just different parts of an area.

## 3. Categorical

This is a very common organizational pattern, and involves separating ideas based on different topics. For example, when discussing the effects of advertising on young children, maybe you can use three categories: the effects on their physical health, the effects on their mental health, and the effects on their intellectual development.

Unit 5  Organizing Speeches

## 4. Cause and Effect

This looks at what has created a problem, and the results of this problem. The cause can be switched in order with the effect, so the effect can be first, and the cause second.

## 5. Problem and Solution

This looks at a problem and offers ways of fixing it. This is a common structure often found in advertisements. An advertisement would begin with a problem that you have (or may not have), and then offer the "solution" which is the product it is selling.

## 6. Compare and Contrast

"Compare" means to show how two or more things are similar. "Contrast" means to show how two or more things are different. The things being compared and contrasted must have some similarities to make this pattern useful. You can choose to only compare, only contrast, or do both.

## 7. Residue

This means looking at eliminating possible ideas one at a time, until the last one must be correct. If you were to choose the most important leader in history, you could look at three possible leaders, and for two of them you could discuss why they are not the most important, which leaves you with only one choice, so that person must be the winner.

**Note:** You can actually mix some patterns. But do consider your thesis statement, general and specific purposes, as well as the audience when mixing organizational patterns. And do not make the speech too complicated or too long.

## Activity 5.2  Matching

### By Yourself

*Read through the examples in Column A and match them to the types in Column B. Draw a line between the items. Then compare your answers with your partner.*

| Column A | Column B |
|---|---|
| (1) I'd like to share with you some insights into what we can all do about it. | (a) Chronological |

(2) Poverty can be caused by a lack of employment in the area. The results are a lower life expectancy, and poorer education.

(3) When men share housework and childcare, their children do better in school... They are less likely to see a child psychiatrist. They are less likely to be put on medication.

(4) In the past, Shenzhen was just a fishing village. Nowadays, it is a major city that is a leader in technology. In the future, it may be a global leader for trade.

(5) The TV series *Journey to the West* is similar to Stephan Chow's movie version in that it tells the story of Monkey. However, Chow's version is different in that it is a comedy.

(6) In today's speech, I am going to discuss the effects of the law for people around the world, people in China, and people in this city.

(7) Which of these three actors is the best? Well, it can't be Tom Hardy as he never won an academy award. It can't be Sandra Bullock as while she has won an academy award, she has also won a Raspberry award for the worst movie. So, it must be Will Smith.

(b) Spatial

(c) Categorical

(d) Cause and effect

(e) Problem and solution

(f) Compare and contrast

(g) Residue

## Activity 5.3  Structuring Main Ideas

### Step 1

### By Yourself

1) Imagine you were to deliver a speech on the topic "Digital Gender Empowerment". You have decided the following points.

(1) General purpose:     Make people feel stronger about a topic.

(2) Specific purpose:     Make people feel stronger about empowering women and girls

# Unit 5  Organizing Speeches

digitally in China.

(3) Thesis statement: It is really important to empower women and girls digitally in China.

*2) Use two from the seven organizational patterns. Briefly outline three main ideas for each organizational pattern you have chosen.*

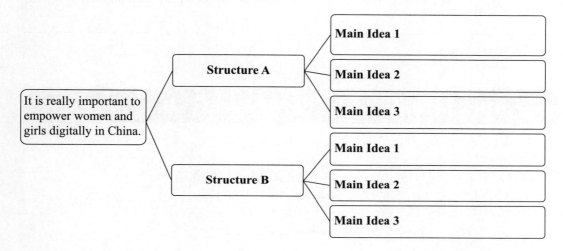

## Step 2

## In Pairs

*Choose the structure plan that you believe is the best for yourself. Take turns reporting the plans you and your partner chose to each other. While listening to your partner, fill in the evaluation table below. Then give your feedbacks to help your partner improve his/her plan.*

| Evaluation | (1) Does his/her organizational pattern match his/her thesis statement and purposes? <br> ☐ Yes ☐ No <br> Because: |
|---|---|
| | (2) Does his/her organizational pattern illustrate his/her main ideas? <br> ☐ Yes ☐ No <br> Because: |

| | (Continued) |
|---|---|
| **Evaluation** | (3) After knowing his/her plan, would you like to hear more about his/her speech?<br>☐ Yes    ☐ No    ☐ Not sure<br>Because: |
| | (4) What else can he/she do to improve his/her organizational plan? |

## 5.4 How to Make Ideas Flow Nicely Using Language?

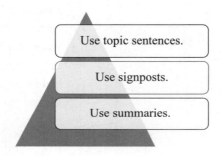

### 1. Use Topic Sentences.

A topic sentence is usually the first sentence of a main idea, that clearly summarizes the main point. A good topic sentence prepares the audience for what is about to happen.

### 2. Use Signposts.

A signpost is a sign of where you are in the speech. Signposts help the audience know what is happening. Some examples are given below:

| Moving onto a New Point | Going into More Detail | Giving Alternatives | Showing Importance | Showing the Part of the Speech |
|---|---|---|---|---|
| • Firstly<br>• Secondly<br>• Onto my next point<br>• Next | • For example<br>• To help you understand<br>• Let's imagine<br>• I want to talk in depth about | • However<br>• In contrast<br>• Nevertheless<br>• Alternatively | • It is crucial that<br>• If you take away one thing from today, it is this<br>• It is vital that<br>• It is really important that | • To begin with<br>• The purpose of my speech is to<br>• To conclude<br>• To summarize my key points |

## 3. Use Summaries.

A conclusion is a summary of all the main ideas, but you can give a short summary at the end of each main idea to help the audience follow (and remember) your arguments.

## Activity 5.4  Designing Body Paragraphs

### By Yourself

*Use the plan you selected in Activity 5.3, and fill in the table below. Once you finish, compare it with your partner to see if your main ideas are nicely structured by your topic sentences and signposts.*

| | |
|---|---|
| **General Purpose:** To make your audience feel stronger about your topic. | |
| **Thesis Statement:** It is really important to empower women and girls digitally in China. | |
| Your choice of organizational structure: _____ | |
| | **Body Structure** |
| **Main Idea 1** | _____ |
| Topic sentence | _____ |
| Type of supporting information | _____ |
| Useful signposts | _____ |
| Summary sentence(s) | _____ |
| | |
| **Main Idea 2** | _____ |
| Topic sentence | _____ |
| Type of supporting information | _____ |
| Useful signposts | _____ |
| Summary sentence(s) | _____ |
| | |
| **Main Idea 3** | _____ |
| Topic sentence | _____ |
| Type of supporting information | _____ |
| Useful signposts | _____ |
| Summary sentence(s) | _____ |

## 5.5 Final Questions

(1) Why is thinking about the structure important to your speech?

(2) What should you consider when choosing the main ideas?

(3) How can you structure the speech with the seven organizational patterns?

(4) How can you make the ideas of your speech flow nicely through the use of language?

# Final Speech Topic

### The Rhetorical Situation

*You are invited to introduce Sustainable Development Goal 5 "Gender Equality" to a group of students from the Department of Gender and Women Studies in UC Berkeley.*

### Step 1

*Read the reports[1] about Sustainable Development Goal 5 "Gender Equality", and discuss the following questions with your partner.*

(1) What is Goal 5?

(2) Why is this goal important?

(3) What are the problems identified in this goal?

 **ACHIEVE GENDER EQUALITY AND EMPOWER ALL WOMEN AND GIRLS**

---

1 The United Nations. 2020. Goal 5: Achieving gender equality. *The United Nations*. Retrieved July 1, 2022, from The United Nations website.
  Anon. 2020. Women's empowerment in the digital age. *The International Telecommunication Union*. Retrieved July 1, 2022, from The International Telecommunication Union website.

Unit 5　Organizing Speeches

## 1. What Is Goal 5?

To achieve gender equality and empower all women and girls.

## 2. Why Is It Important? What Are the Issues Addressed by This Goal?

Women and girls represent half of the world's population and therefore also half of its potential. But today gender inequality persists everywhere and slows down the social progress. Women continue to be underrepresented at all levels of political leadership. Across the globe, women and girls perform a much higher share of unpaid domestic work. Inequalities faced by women and girls may begin right at birth and follow them all their lives. In some countries, women and girls are not given much access to health care or proper nutrition, leading to a higher mortality rate.

### Step 2

*You are about to read a description of digital empowerment and its importance as suggested by the Beijing Declaration and Platform for Action. Read it through and discuss the following questions with your partner.*

(1) What does empowerment mean in terms of gender equality?

(2) Why is digital empowerment important?

## 3. What Is Empowerment?

Empowerment means the act of empowering someone; the granting of the power, right, or authority to perform various acts or duties.[1]

Guaranteeing the rights of women and girls and giving them opportunities to reach their full potential are critical not only for attaining gender equality, but also for meeting a wide range of international development goals. Empowered women and girls contribute to the health and productivity of their families, communities, and countries. Women's (or girls') empowerment is fostering a woman's (or girl's) sense of worth, her decision-making power, her access to opportunities and resources, her power and control over her life inside and outside the home, and her ability to effect change.[2]

---

1　Anon. 2020. Definition of "empowerment". *Merriam-Webster Dictionary*. Retrieved June 30, 2022, from Merriam-Webster website.

2　Anon. 2020. Global issues: Gender equality and women's empowerment. *Peace Corps*. Retrieved June 30, 2022, from Peace Corps website.

## 4. What Is Digital Empowerment?

As one of the sub-goals of SDG 5, digital empowerment basically means to enhance the use of enabling technology, in particular information and communications technology, to promote the empowerment of women.

## 5. Why Is Digital Empowerment Important for Gender Equality?

The Beijing Declaration and Platform for Action called for the full and equal participation of women in and through media and new technologies of communication; yet, it was estimated that 200 million fewer women than men around the world have Internet access—and the digital gender gap may well be widening. Given that over 95% of jobs today have a digital component, if women are not adequately trained, they will have reduced access to employment and will face social exclusion (being left behind in a progress).

### Step 3

*With the notes from your reading and discussion, prepare a speech based on the rhetorical situation given in this unit. Pay attention to topic sentences and signposts which would help make your speech flow nicely.*

# Unit 6
## Beginning and Ending Speeches

# OBJECTIVES

After studying this unit, you should be able to:

(1) Understand the importance and structure of introductions and conclusions.

(2) Practice on how to begin your speech, especially in relation to getting the attention of the audience.

(3) Practice on how to end your speech.

# Warm Up

## In Pairs

*Discuss the following questions with your partner.*

(1) What type of job do you want to get after graduation?

(2) What do you need to do during university in order to get your dream job?

Unit 6　Beginning and Ending Speeches

## 6.1　Why Is an Introduction Important to a Speech?

The introduction of a speech is important for the following reasons.

## 1. It Gets the Attention of the Audience.

A good introduction grabs the audience's attention and interest. It makes them want to listen to your speech. Compare the following two beginnings. Which one makes you want to listen for more?

   (1) Nice to meet you guys in this forum. Today, I'd like to share some Chinese poverty eradication experience, and hope my talk will bring some inspiring ideas to you.

   (2) I grew up in a small, run-down fishing village. Back then... But now, if you visited my hometown, you would find... Yes, it is now a holiday resort. All of these changes are due to the policy—Paired Assistance.

## 2. It Can Influence How the Audience Feel About You.

In the introduction, you can establish why you are the right person to speak about this topic. This can be very important in building credibility. Also, you can use the information from your audience analysis to start to tailor the speech to their needs.

## 3. It Informs the Audience What the Speech Will Be About.

While the title of the speech often gives a good hint, the introduction is your chance to inform the audience exactly about what you are going to do with the speech, that is, the thesis statement.

## 4. It Previews and Shows the Structural Plan of the Speech.

A good speech is easy to follow. The introduction allows you to explain to the audience your plan for the speech so that they are prepared for what you will say.

## Activity 6.1  Collecting Information

### In Pairs

*What are the things your university is doing to help you be prepared for finding a job after graduation? Go to your university's website and look for the relevant information. A common place for this kind of information would be the Student Employment Office. Fill in the table below and then share the information you have found with your partner.*

| What Are the Services Provided? | How Can They Help You Find a Job? |
|---|---|
|  |  |

## 6.2  How to Structure the Introduction of a Speech?

There are mainly four steps to structure the introduction of a speech:

### 1. Getting the Attention of the Audience.

You need to get your audience's attention from the very beginning in your speech. If they are not interested at the beginning, they may not be interested at the end. In public speeches, there are some techniques that will serve as attention grabbers. We will examine them later.

### 2. Stating the Thesis Statement.

After the attention grabber, your introduction should provide the thesis statement. Since it appears for the first time in your speech, don't be vague. It has to be as simple and clear as possible. You can now go to Activity 6.4 and check again your thesis statement for its clarity.

### 3. Establishing Your Credibility.

A credible speaker means someone who is trustworthy as a speaker. The audience would tend to believe what a credible speaker is going to say. Even if you are not an expert on a topic, you need to show that you know this topic from your research and your own experience.

Unit 6　Beginning and Ending Speeches

## 4. Outlining the Speech.

The final part of your introduction is to outline the speech. This means to tell your audience what your main ideas are, and how they are structured logically. So, check your answers in Activity 6.2 to see if the main ideas can support your main thesis, and if they are well connected.

## Activity 6.2　Structuring an Introduction

### Step 1

### By Yourself

*Make a speech according to the following information.*

| |
|---|
| **Topic:** How Chinese universities promote youth employment. |
| **General Purpose:** To give people new information. |
| **Specific Purpose:** To let people know how Chinese college students are supported by their universities for starting their businesses. |
| **Audience:** Students of your university who want to create their own businesses. |

| | |
|---|---|
| What is your thesis statement? | |
| Why should the audience listen to you? | |
| What would be the plan of your main ideas? (See Activity 6.1, but feel free to add new ideas here.) | |
| What organizational structure can work well here? (**Note:** You can choose more than one.) | ☐ Chronological <br> ☐ Spatial <br> ☐ Categorical <br> ☐ Cause and effect <br> ☐ Problem and solution <br> ☐ Compare and contrast <br> ☐ Residue |

**Step 2**

**In Pairs**

*Based on your work in the table above, discuss your answers to the following questions with your partner. Then try to offer some suggestions to help your partner improve his/her plan.*

(1) Is the thesis statement specific or vague? Is it relevant to the topic and purposes?

(2) Did you successfully prove to be trustworthy on the topic? If not, how can you improve it?

(3) Did the speech preview demonstrate a clear structure of the main ideas?

## 6.3 How to Get the Audience's Attention?

Here is a list of attention grabbers commonly used in public speaking.

## 1. Use the Speech Situation Itself.

Use the speech situation itself to begin your speech. For example, if you were giving a speech at a celebration of promotion to a co-worker, you could refer to the co-worker, the promotion, the date and the company.

## 2. Build a Relationship with the Audience.

A second way of introducing your speech is to build a relationship with the audience. You could relate the topic to the audience in some way, or try to find something in common between yourself and the audience.

## 3. Discuss the Importance of Your Topic.

You could directly discuss the importance of your topic. Just tell the audience that the topic is vital, and they need to listen for their own good.

## 4. Tell the Audience the Purpose of Your Speech.

You can tell the audience the purpose of your speech. If you inform them of your specific purpose, they may be convinced and listen for more details.

## 5. Use Statistics.

The use of statistics that are shocking may surprise the audience and make them want to know more. However, you need to be as accurate as possible for establishing credibility; meanwhile, accurate numbers might still be doubted by the audience. So, be aware of this when using this tactic.

## 6. Tell a Story.

A story can be a really good way of getting the audience to listen to you. A good story can really "paint a picture" for the audience.

## 7. Use an Analogy.

An analogy is comparing two completely different things in order to make a difficult thing easier to understand. For example, "Life is like a box of chocolates—You never know what you're gonna get!" In this analogy, the complex issue of how life can be random is compared to a simple item of a box of chocolates.

## 8. Use a Rhetorical Question.

You can just ask the audience a question. This can be useful to get the audience to imagine a situation, or to think back to their experiences.

## 9. Use a Quote.

A quote is using words from an expert, a famous person, or somebody related to the topic. If you begin the speech with someone's quote, make sure that this person is relevant to your speech.

## 10. Use Humor.

Humor can be a good way of encouraging people to listen, and can surprise people, especially those who may disagree with your topic and purpose.

# Activity 6.3  Matching

# By Yourself

*Match the examples in Column A to the attention grabbers in Column B.*

**Column A**

(1) Have you traveled by plane, train and car? Which form of transport do you prefer?

(2) People who are caught drink driving have, on average, driven 80 times drunk before being caught.

(3) The purpose of this speech is to encourage all of you to start saving for retirement.

(4) In 2011, I was in Sendai, Japan when the tsunami hit. Here, I want to tell you how to survive a tsunami.

(5) Welcome everyone. On this day in 1949, the People's Republic of China was formed. Therefore, in this speech I want to discuss how we arrived at this point, and what the future holds for China.

(6) In 2010, Xi Jinping said "It was the greatest contribution towards the whole of human race, made by China, that is to prevent its 1.3 billion people from hunger."

(7) Many of you, as students, have experienced what it is like to have to leave home in order to fulfill a dream. It is hard, it is scary, and it causes sadness. Another person who has felt the exact same way in trying to achieve his dream is…

(8) The environment is possibly one of the most important topics of discussion today, which scientists say can impact future generations.

**Column B**

(a) Use the speech situation itself.

(b) Build a relationship with the audience.

(c) Discuss the importance of your topic.

(d) Tell the audience the purpose of your speech.

(e) Use statistics.

(f) Use a rhetorical question.

(g) Use a quote.

(h) Tell a story.

Unit 6   Beginning and Ending Speeches

## Activity 6.4   Choosing Your Attention Grabber

### Step 1

### By Yourself

*Based on your work on Activity 6.3, choose three styles of attention grabbers that you can use in your speech. Then make some brief notes on how you will use them.*

|  | Attention Grabber 1 | Attention Grabber 2 | Attention Grabber 3 |
|---|---|---|---|
| **How Will You Use It?** |  |  |  |

### Step 2

### By Yourself

*Choose an attention grabber from Step 1 and write it out in full below.*

    (1) Attention grabber: _____

    (2) Your writing: _____

### Step 3

### In Pairs

*Compare your final attention grabber with your partner. Which idea do you like? What suggestions do you have to make it even better?*

## Activity 6.5   Bringing It All Together (1)

### By Yourself

*Using your information from Activity 6.1 to Activity 6.4, write down your introduction in full. You should pay attention to the following points.*

    (1) Get the attention of the audience. (**Note:** You can use your writing from Activity 6.4.)

    (2) State the thesis statement.

    (3) Establish your credibility.

    (4) Outline the speech.

    (5) Use signposts.

## 6.4　How to Structure the Conclusion of a Speech?

A conclusion is essential in a speech for the following reasons.

## 1. Signal the End of the Talk.

A well-organized speech with proper "signposts" will be clear in the stage of the presentation. So to signal the end of a speech, phrases or "signposts" such as "To end my speech", "To conclude what I have said", and "In summary" are often used.

## 2. Help People Remember the Key Points.

It can be difficult for the audience to remember all main ideas, so the conclusion is a chance for you to bring everything together.

## 3. Leave the Audience with Something to Think About.

A good conclusion can make your speech memorable and therefore gives you a greater chance to achieve your aims.

Below is a flow chart showing you how a conclusion is structured:

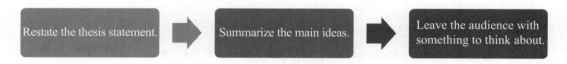

## 1. Restate the Thesis Statement.

After signposting the conclusion, by saying "in conclusion" or "to sum up" for example, the first thing is to restate the thesis statement. In your introduction, you would have told the audience the thesis statement, you will need to do it again here as it leads nicely into the second part of the conclusion—summarizing the main ideas. Do not use the same words from the thesis statement as you have used in the introduction; change the words a bit.

## 2. Summarize the Main Ideas.

This will help the audience remember the key points. Be specific with your summary, and include all of the main points. Your conclusion must be understandable on its own.

# Unit 6 Beginning and Ending Speeches

## 3. Leave the Audience with Something to Think About.

This can be done in many ways, as shown below:

**Refer back to the introduction.**
- If you asked some rhetorical questions, or told a story in the introduction, then in the conclusion, you can go back to these questions or the story and discuss them again, but with new knowledge from your speech to show how things can be different with this new knowledge.

**Challenge the audience.**
- If you want the audience to do something, maybe you can challenge them by giving them a task to complete.

**Give a utopian future.**
- Give the audience a picture of a perfect world in the future, and how your arguments can help make this perfect world.

## Activity 6.6 Choosing Your Conclusion

### Step 1

### In Pairs

*Use the questions below to discuss three ways you can leave the audience with something to think about.*

| Types of Conclusions | Questions for You to Consider |
|---|---|
| Use a quote. | What kind of person will be a good person to quote for this speech? Why? What kind of information can you quote? |
| Challenge the audience. | How can you use your conclusion to challenge your audience? |
| Give a utopian future. | Suppose you benefited from being a student-entrepreneur. How can you turn these elements into a conclusion that offers a utopian, positive future to your audience? |

**Step 2**

## In Pairs

*Choose one type from Step 1, and write it out in full below.*

(1) Your choice: _____

(2) Your writing: _____

### Activity 6.7　Bringing It All Together (2)

## By Yourself

*Using your information from Activity 6.6, write down your conclusion in full. You should pay attention to the following points.*

(1) Restate the thesis statement.

(2) Summarize the main ideas.

(3) Leave the audience with something to think about.

(4) Use signposts.

## 6.5　Final Questions

(1) Why is it important to have a good introduction and conclusion in a speech?

(2) How can you begin a speech? What is the structure of an introduction?

(3) What is an attention grabber?

(4) What types of attention grabbers are there?

(5) How can you end a speech? What is the structure of a conclusion?

Unit 6   Beginning and Ending Speeches

# Final Speech Topic

## The Rhetorical Situation

*You are invited to give a talk at the Decent Work Awareness Event, organized by the Beijing Office of the UN agency, International Labor Organization (ILO). ILO's job in China focuses on employment creation, and the audience want to know what methods China has taken to create employment. You are to inform them of China's methods in creating employment among college students in particular, and how Chinese college students are supported for starting their businesses.*

### Step 1

*Read the reports[1] about Sustainable Development Goal 8 "Decent Work and Economic Growth", and discuss the following questions with your partner.*

    (1) What is addressed in Goal 8?

    (2) What is decent work?

    (3) Why is this goal important?

    (4) What can be done to achieve this goal?

 **PROMOTE SUSTAINED, INCLUSIVE AND SUSTAINABLE ECONOMIC GROWTH, FULL AND PRODUCTIVE EMPLOYMENT AND DECENT WORK FOR ALL**

## 1. What Is Goal 8?

It is to promote long-term and worker-friendly economic growth, employment and decent work for all. Decent work means opportunities for everyone to get work that is productive and delivers a fair income, security in the workplace and social protection for families, better

---

1 The United Nations. 2020. Goal 8: Decent work and economic growth. *The United Nations*. Retrieved February 21, 2022, from The United Nations website.
The International Labor Organization. 2020. Decent work. *The International Labor Organization*. Retrieved February 22, 2022, from The International Labor Organization website.

prospects for personal development and social integration.

## 2. Why Is It Important?

Economic growth needs to be long-term and worker-friendly, so that it can create decent jobs for all and improve living standards. However, since 2020, our economic and financial situations became worse due to the pandemic. For instance, the number of jobs lost during 2020 is four times more than the lost during the global financial crisis (2007–2009).

## 3. What Can Be Done?

It is needed to provide the youth the best opportunities to find decent jobs. This calls for investing in education and training of the highest possible quality, providing young people with skills that match with the job market demands, and making the situation fair and balanced so that all aspiring youth can attain productive employment regardless of their gender, income level and social background.

## Step 2

*You are about to read how China promotes youth employment while they are still at college. Read the following passage and discuss the questions with your partner.*

(1) What are China's methods to increase employment for college students?

(2) How does this help the country achieve Goal 8?

In 2021, the General Office of the State Council (国务院) in China issued a guideline[1]

---

[1] The State Council of the People's Republic of China. 2021. More support for college students starting businesses. *The State Council of the People's Republic of China*. Retrieved March 6, 2022, from The State Council of the People's Republic of China website.

# Unit 6  Beginning and Ending Speeches

to maximize the opportunity for college students to transition to decent jobs. Universities are to help students in the following aspects:

| | |
|---|---|
| **On-campus Training** | (1) Find mentors for students to encourage innovation and entrepreneurship.<br>(2) Hold activities on campus to reward and promote innovation.<br>(3) Encourage participation in Students' "Internet Plus" Innovation and Entrepreneurship Competitions（"互联网+"创新创业大赛）. |
| **University Services** | (1) Provide working space to encourage students to work together to create new business ideas.<br>(2) Share innovation resources such as labs, equipment and facilities and offer cheap, high-quality professional services.<br>(3) Launch cooperation between universities and businesses to promote entrepreneurship and employment.<br>(4) Provide students with accurate information on industrial developments and market trends. |

## Step 3

*With the notes from your reading and discussion, prepare a speech based on the rhetorical situation given in this unit. Pay attention to the designing of your introduction and conclusion, by following the steps described in this unit.*

# Unit 7
# Creating Speech Outlines

# OBJECTIVES

After studying this unit, you should be able to:

(1) Know what a speech outline looks like.

(2) Understand why developing an outline is essential for preparing and delivering a speech.

(3) Create an outline using all methods discussed in this book.

# Warm Up

## In Pairs

***Choose one topic below, and discuss it with your partner.***

**Topic 1:** Imagine there was no tap water service in your area. What difficulties may you encounter?

**Topic 2:** Do you know where the tap water you use comes from? How many water purification factories are there in the place where you live now?

Unit 7   Creating Speech Outlines

## 7.1  What Is a Speech Outline?

A speech outline is the structure of what you are going to say; it is a plan of your speech. It is a one- or two-page document that shows what and how you will discuss about the topic. The following is an example:

---

**Speech Outline Illustration**

Analysis of the Rhetorical Situation: _____

Analysis of the Audience: _____

Topic: _____

General Purpose: _____

Specific Purpose: _____

[*Look at your audience; smile*]

**Introduction**

• Attention Grabber: _____

• Thesis Statement: _____

• Establish Credibility: _____

• Preview of Main Points: _____

**Body**

• Main Point 1: _____

    Supporting Material 1

    Supporting Material 2

• Main Point 2: _____

    Supporting Material 1

    Supporting Material 2

...

[*Signal the end; pause*]

**Conclusion**

• Restate the Thesis Statement: _____

• Summary of Main Ideas: _____

• Leave the Audience with Something to Think About: _____

This outline includes basically everything we have studied and are going to study in this book. The following tree map will give you a general picture of these elements, and also the steps for creating an outline:

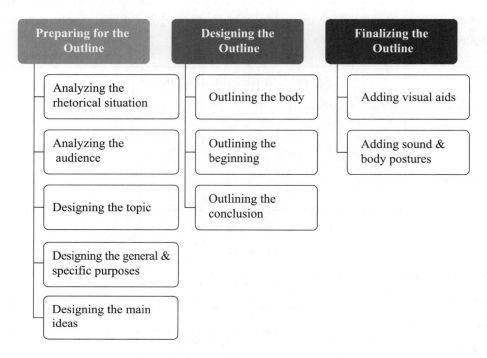

## 7.2 Why Do You Need an Outline?

Building up an outline can help you:

(1) Plan your speech.

(2) Examine your speech for improvements.

(3) Give you notes to refer to during speaking.

(4) Apply all you have studied in this book.

Unit 7  Creating Speech Outlines

## 7.3 How to Create an Outline?

How can you create an outline? That is the focus of this unit. It may seem scary, but you have covered (or will look at) all of these before. Now you are just putting them all together. The following flow chart gives you a basic idea of the methods and steps of designing an outline. The rest of this unit will guide you step by step to build up an outline.

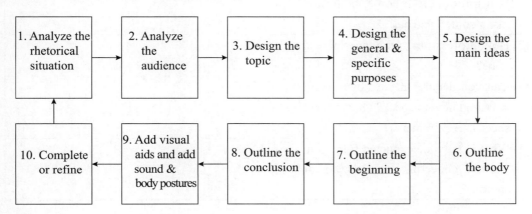

### Activity 7.1  Analyzing the Situation (See Unit 1)

*Planning a speech often begins with analyzing the rhetorical situation. You need to examine what the rhetorical situation is in order to deliver a speech that is expected. Now, imagine that you were going to make a speech according to the following information.*

| |
|---|
| **Topic:** Youth Participation in Promoting Clean Water Accessibility |
| **General purpose:** To give people new information. |
| **Specific purpose:** To let the audience know what young Chinese people are doing to promote the access to clean water in rural areas and help the locals get clean water. |
| **Audience:** 8 professors and 89 students from the Department of Environmental Science who are interested in how clean water is promoted in rural places. |

## In Pairs

*Work with your partner and write your answers to the questions below. Consider how the analysis results may affect your plan of the speech.*

| Guiding Questions | Your Answers | How Will It Affect Your Speech? |
|---|---|---|
| (1) Where does the speech take place? Is it informal like home, or formal like a conference hall? | | |
| (2) How professional are you expected to be? | | |
| (3) Can you decide on your own about what and how to speak? Or, are there specific requirements? | | |
| (4) What is the tone expected from you, excited, cheerful, worried, sad, or anxious? | | |

## Activity 7.2  Analyzing the Audience (See Unit 2)

## In Pairs

*Audience analysis is key to your entire speech. The results from the analysis should also be kept in front of you throughout the whole outlining process. Now, read again the speech description above to learn more about your audience. Work with your partner and answer the questions below.*

| Guiding Questions | Your Answers | How Will It Affect Your Speech? |
|---|---|---|
| (1) How many people will be your audience? | | |
| (2) Do people want to be your audience? | | |
| (3) What are the characteristics of your audience?<br>• Age<br>• Gender<br>• Income<br>• Education | | |

# Unit 7  Creating Speech Outlines

(Continued)

| Guiding Questions | Your Answers | How Will It Affect Your Speech? |
|---|---|---|
| (4) Is your speech online or in front of your audience? | | |
| (5) How diverse are your audience? | | |
| (6) What are the stereotypes of the audience you should avoid? | | |
| (7) What do your audience know about the topic? | | |
| (8) How can you make sure the audience get the message that you want them to (i.e. reducing noise)? | | |

## Activity 7.3  Designing the General and Specific Purposes (See Unit 3)

### In Pairs

*1) Read the topic and purposes of your speech again. Work in pairs and choose another one or even more general purposes from the list below.*

| General Purpose List | Your Choice and Reason |
|---|---|
| (1) Make people feel good or bad about something. | ☐ |
| (2) Make people start talking about something. | ☐ |
| (3) Give new information. | ☑ |
| (4) Change people's opinion completely. | ☐ |
| (5) Make people feel weaker about something. | ☐ |
| (6) Make people feel stronger about something. | ☐ |
| (7) Make people do something. | ☐ |

*2) Now, use what you chose as general purposes and decide on the specific purposes.*

   **[E.g.]** <u>Give new information</u>: Give new information to senior citizens about how clean water is supplied in the local community.

   (1) General purposes: _____

   (2) Specific purposes: _____

# Activity 7.4  Designing the Main Ideas (See Unit 5)

*For the main ideas, you can focus on the following three points.*

(1) Talk about what problems there are with accessing to clean water in the world today.

(2) Talk about what people can do to promote clean water accessibility.

(3) Talk about how civil society organizations (民间社会团体) have been engaging young people and the rural community to provide clean water to the locals.

## By Yourself

*To learn more about the situation of clean water usage today, read the UN report on Goal 6 at the end of this unit. Make some notes from your reading for main ideas. Then fill in the box below.*

| Main Idea Box |
|---|
| (1) For describing the situation of clean water accessibility today: <br> [Key words] |
| (2) For introducing what can be done to promote clean water accessibility: <br> [Key words] |
| (3) For explaining how young people have been engaged with promoting clean water accessibility: <br> [Key words] |

## In Pairs

*Compare your notes with your partner, and discuss the main ideas you chose and the links between them.*

| Note Box |
|---|
|  |

Unit 7  Creating Speech Outlines

## Activity 7.5  Outlining the Body

### Step 1  Organizing the Structure (See Unit 3)

**By Yourself**

1) Refer back to the three main ideas in Activity 7.4. Which organizational structure will you use to fulfill your speech purposes (see Activity 7.3)?

| Organizational Patterns | | | |
|---|---|---|---|
| Chronological | Spatial | Categorical | Cause and effect |
| Problem and solution | Compare and contrast | Residue | |
| **Your Choice** | | | |
| **Reasons** | | | |

**In Pairs**

2) Explain to your partner why you chose that particular organizational pattern.

### Step 2  Locating Supporting Information (See Unit 4)

*When choosing supporting information, you need to consider the materials that can directly back up the idea, without your audience spending too much effort on guessing and inferring. Remember to make a reference to where you get the information. Now, focus on Main Idea 3 in Activity 7.4. In order to make it more convincing to the audience, you need to back it up with supporting materials.*

| Main Idea 3 |
|---|
| The ways civil society organizations have been engaging young people and the rural community to provide clean water to the locals. |

**In Pairs**

*Search online for information concerning MyH2O. A brief summary of the organization can also be found at the end of this unit. What materials can you find that will be useful to*

support the main idea above? Work in pairs and write down the supporting information, and identify what type it is.

| Personal experience | Observations | Examples |
| Common knowledge | Documents | Statistics |
| Testimony | | |

| Main Idea 3 | Civil society organizations have been engaging young people and the rural community to promote access to safe drinking water. |
|---|---|
| Supporting Information 1 | |
| Supporting Information 2 | |
| Supporting Information 3 | |

## Activity 7.6  Outlining the Beginning (See Unit 6)

### In Pairs

*Fill in the table below for what you believe would be a good introduction for the situation, audience, and speech purposes. A list of attention grabbers is provided below.*

| Attention Grabbers | |
|---|---|
| Use the speech situation itself. | Build a relationship with the audience. |
| Discuss the importance of your topic. | Tell the audience the purpose of your speech. |
| Use statistics. | Tell a story. |
| Use an analogy. | Use a rhetorical question. |
| Use a quote. | Use humor. |

| Introduction | • Attention grabber:<br><br>• Thesis statement:<br><br>• Establishing credibility:<br><br>• Plan of the speech: |
|---|---|

Unit 7   Creating Speech Outlines

## Activity 7.7   Outlining the Conclusion (See Unit 6)

### In Pairs

*Use the following guiding questions for outlining the conclusion, and fill in the table below.*

(1) What was the thesis statement of your speech?

(2) What were the main points mentioned in your speech?

(3) How will you leave the audience something to think about?

| Strategies |
|---|
| Use a quote.                              Give a utopian future.<br>Challenge the audience. |

| | |
|---|---|
| Conclusion | • Restating the thesis statement:<br><br>• Summarizing main points:<br><br>• Leaving something for the audience to think about: |

## Activity 7.8   Adding Visuals, Voice and Postures (See Unit 10)

### By Yourself

*The last step in planning your outline is to make a note on what visual aids you can use, and what you can do with your voice, body, etc. so as to make the speech more interesting and understandable to your audience. These will be covered in Unit 10.*

## 7.4   Final Questions

(1) What does a speech outline look like?

(2) Why is it important to create an outline?

(3) What steps are there to follow when you design a speech outline?

# Final Speech Topic

### The Rhetorical Situation

*You are a UN youth delegate from China, involved in promoting the awareness concerning Sustainable Development Goal 6 "Clean Water and Sanitation". You are to speak at the Global Youth Summit held by the United Nations Educational, Scientific and Cultural Organization (UNESCO). You are to talk about how young people in China are promoting clean water accessibility. The Summit is held at Hawaii University to a group of 50 international student attendants from all over the world who are all interested in the topic. For this purpose, you plan to use MyH2O as an example, and deliver a speech focusing on describing Goal 6 as a background framework, introducing the initiatives (倡议) set up by Goal 6, and how MyH2O has been engaging with rural communities to promote access to safe drinking water. Follow the instruction below to work on your outline of the speech.*

## Step 1

*Read the reports[1] about Sustainable Development Goal 6 "Clean Water and Sanitation", and discuss the following questions with your partner.*

    (1) What is addressed in Goal 6?

    (2) Why is this goal important?

    (3) What are the problems identified in this goal?

    (4) What can be done to achieve this goal, and by whom?

---

1 The United Nations. 2020. Goal 6: Clean water and sanitation. *The United Nations*. Retrieved April 12, 2022, from The United Nations website.
   World Health Organization. 2022. Drinking water. *WHO*. Retrieved April 12, 2022, from WHO website.

Unit 7　Creating Speech Outlines

## ENSURE AVAILABILITY AND SUSTAINABLE MANAGEMENT OF WATER AND SANITATION FOR ALL

### 1. What Is Goal 6?

It is to make sure that by 2030, all people can have the access to safe and affordable drinking water and sanitation.

### 2. Why Is It Important? What Issues Are There Related to This Goal?

Everyone is entitled to water that is from an improved water source, and can obtain it easily when needed, and free from chemical contamination. Nevertheless, people are facing growing challenges related to water scarcity and pollution. First, the demand for water is more than the growth of population. Half of the world's population has already been experiencing serious water scarcity at least one month a year. Meanwhile, people who live in rural areas or cities with low income usually have less access to improved sources of drinking water than other residents.

### 3. What Can Be Done?

The UN encourages more civil society organizations to work together with governments in water research and development. Also, these organizations should welcome more women, young people and the locals to participate in promoting local access to clean water.

### Step 2

*Read the following passage about MyH2O and discuss the questions with your partner.*

　　(1) How does the organization operate to tackle the issues mentioned in Goal 6?

　　(2) How does the organization engage young people in achieving Goal 6?

In China, MyH2O is a data platform that includes a mobile phone APP. This APP allows rural residents to know where to find clean water and connects communities with private companies and non-profit organizations that provide effective water solutions. The running of MyH2O relies on a nationwide network of youth volunteers who are trained to test water quality and log their results into the interactive platform. Ren is the founder of MyH2O, and was named a Young Champion of the Earth by the United Nations Environment Program[1]. As a civil society organization, MyH2O has been founded and run by young people, and is also engaging hundreds of university students each year in promoting clean water accessibility.

## Step 3

*With the notes from your reading and discussion, prepare a speech based on the rhetorical situation given in this unit. You can also use all your notes from all the activities covered earlier in this unit.*

---

1 Young Champion of the Earth. 2020. Turning data into drinking water in China. *Young Champion of the Earth*. Retrieved June 30, 2022, from Young Champion of the Earth website.

# Unit 8 Giving Informative Speeches

# OBJECTIVES

After studying this unit, you should be able to:

(1) Understand what an informative speech is.

(2) Identify the speech purposes which can be achieved through informative speeches.

(3) Learn the informative strategies of defining, reporting, describing, explaining, and comparing.

(4) Know how to plan for an informative speech.

# Warm Up

**ERADICATION OF POVERTY**

## In Pairs

*Discuss the following questions about poverty with your partner. Try to explore the reasons behind your partner's answers.*

(1) What is poverty? What does it mean to you?

(2) Can you use examples, including personal experiences, stories, news, and other forms of information to explain your understanding of poverty?

Unit 8   Giving Informative Speeches

## 8.1   What Is an Informative Speech?

An informative speech is a speech that provides the audience with what they do not know, or you thought they know but are actually wrong. Normally, informative speeches are ones that share information about objects, processes, events and ideas. The following shows what an informative speech can do:

(1) Provide new information or share a new perspective.

(2) Set the agenda and make people start talking.

(3) Intensify or weaken a feeling.

## 8.2   How to Design an Informative Speech?

A speech is designed to meet a purpose. In order to fulfill the purposes above, certain informative strategies could be used to design your informative speeches. These strategies can help specify your purposes, and also plan your informative speeches in a more structural and effective way. There are five types of informative strategies:

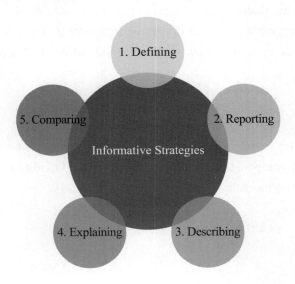

## 1. Defining

Defining means to give information that helps clarify an idea, a concept or a term in your speech. Giving definition can also be used to introduce a new way of viewing things. For example, poverty can be defined from the perspective of money, living condition, or access to basic living materials.

## 2. Reporting

Reporting means to describe what happened. Reporting is often used for informing an event, an experience, or a person—just like what journalism does.

## 3. Describing

Describing means to paint a mental picture in your audience's minds. You commonly describe a person's outlook, an object, or a place with detailed information. Describing is useful when you want to avoid generalization and want the audience to have more details about the topic.

## 4. Explaining

Explaining is more than defining a term or making an idea precise and clear. Explaining means to share with your audience a deeper understanding of events, people, policies or processes. It involves explaining how they happened, why they happened, and what they mean or imply.

## 5. Comparing

Comparing means to clarify for the audience the similarities and differences between the things that are being compared. The purpose of comparing is either to make the two things more similar, or more different than the audience had imagined.

# Unit 8  Giving Informative Speeches

## Activity 8.1  Matching

### By Yourself

*Match the speaking performances in Column A to the types of informative speeches in Column B.*

| Column A | Column B |
| --- | --- |
| (1) To describe to your audience the process used to build a house. | (a) Defining |
| (2) To describe to your audience the geographical varieties of your hometown. | (b) Reporting |
| (3) To describe to your audience the life of a senior member of your family. | (c) Describing |
| (4) To describe what "financial bubble" in the world's economy is. | (d) Explaining |
| (5) To describe how informative speeches are different from persuasive speeches. | (e) Comparing |

## Activity 8.2  Planning with Informative Strategies

The five mini-activities below will help you learn how to use the five informative strategies discussed in 8.2. Follow the steps and complete the tasks.

### Step 1  Defining

### By Yourself

*In Warm Up, you learnt the definition of poverty. Now, write two definitions of poverty that can allow you to see this topic in two different ways.*

(1) Definition 1: _____

(2) Definition 2: _____

### Step 2  Reporting

### In Pairs

*Think of a time when you saw on social media or in real life a person or group of people*

living in poverty. Imagine yourself a journalist, and take some notes as to what happened such as the major activities that took place at the scene. Then share this by reporting it to your partner with the help of your notes.

**Note Box**

### Step 3   Describing

## In Pairs

*Use one of the two pictures on the next page. Focus on the place or a person in the picture and describe as many details as possible. Try to relate the details to poverty alleviation—how poverty can be reduced by the object or the activity the person is engaged with in the picture. Then share this by describing it to your partner with the help of your notes.*

| Picture | Description of Details |
|---|---|
|  |  |

### Step 4   Explaining

## In Pairs

*Use the same picture above and explain what happened in this picture, what policies are taken for it to happen, and what it implies or suggests to the rest of the world with regard to poverty reduction. Then share this by explaining it to your partner with the help of your notes.*

Unit 8　Giving Informative Speeches

| Explanation |
|---|
| • What has happened in this picture? |
| • What are the policies taken for it to happen? |
| • What does it imply? |

## Step 5　Comparing

## By Yourself

*According to the World Bank, women represent a majority of the poor in many regions[1]. So the focus of the work often lies on empowering women with the skills to work and to earn money on their own. Compare the two pictures below that show women working. Describe how one picture is similar to and different from the other.*

　　**Note:** The goal of this comparison is to heighten the audience's awareness of similarity—the importance of women empowerment in poverty reduction.

　　(1) What are the similarities shown in the two pictures above?

　　(2) What are the differences shown in the two pictures above?

　　(3) What do these similarities and differences suggest in terms of poverty alleviation?

---

1　The World Bank. 2022. Understanding poverty: Overview. *The World Bank.* Retrieved October 21, 2022, from The World Bank website.

# Activity 8.3　Planning an Informative Speech

*Now, you will go through the process of making an informative speech with the following scenario. Have a look at your answers to Activity 8.2. How can you use each of the informative strategies in the speech task below? The complete rhetorical situation of this task can be found at the end of this unit.*

**Note:** The aim here is to give you choices. By looking at each type of informative speeches, you can see the options you have and this can give you creativity.

| Your Topic | How China has managed to eradicate extreme poverty. |
|---|---|
| Your General Purposes | • To make people feel stronger about something.<br>• To give people new information. |
| Your Specific Purposes | • To let people become aware that poverty is extreme.<br>• To let people know how China has managed to eradicate extreme poverty. |
| Your Audience | 35 university attendees from East Asian countries at the Economic and Social Council Youth Forum. |

## Step 1　Design Main Ideas

## In Pairs

The main ideas can cover two aspects:

(1) What is extreme poverty?

　• Defining extreme poverty.

　• Why is it so urgent to end extreme poverty?

(2) Describing China's anti-poverty methods.

　• What methods has China taken to end extreme poverty?

　• What do these methods imply?

*Use your notes from the five informative strategies above and fill in the box on the next page. Remember to adapt your definition according to your rhetorical situation, audience and purposes. Compare your notes with your partner.*

Unit 8  Giving Informative Speeches

---

**1. What is extreme poverty?**

1.1 Defining extreme poverty.

1.2 Why is it so urgent to end extreme poverty?

---

### Step 2   Outline the Body

## 1. Organizational Structure

### By Yourself

*Choose an organizational structure from below and write down the reasons for your choice. Then compare your notes with your partner. When you choose, consider the following questions.*

(1) What organizational structure do you think is the most effective to arrange the above points 1.1 and 1.2?

(2) To what extent does this structure fulfill the general and specific purposes of your informative speech?

| Organizational Patterns | Chronological | Spatial | Categorical | Cause and effect |
|---|---|---|---|---|
| | Problem and solution | Compare and contrast | Residue | |
| Your Choice | | | | |
| Your Reasons | | | | |

## 2. Supporting Information

### In Pairs

1) At the end of this unit, you can find some materials that can be used as supporting information. Collect supporting materials to back up your idea on Main Idea 2 in Activity 8.3, "What did China do to end extreme poverty?" Work in pairs and answer the following questions.

| Personal experience | Observations | Examples |
|---|---|---|
| Common knowledge | Documents | Statistics |
| Testimony | | |

| Student A | Student B |
|---|---|
| Read the article in Appendix and answer the question:<br><br>(2.1) What methods has China taken to end extreme poverty? | Read the article in Appendix and answer the question:<br><br>(2.2) What do these methods imply? |
| [List the sub-ideas with supporting materials] | [List the sub-ideas with supporting materials] |

*2) Now, compare your two lists with your partner and complete Main Idea 2 in Activity 8.3 with the organizational structure you have chosen.*

## 8.3 Final Questions

(1) What is an informative speech?

(2) What are the purposes achieved through informative speeches?

(3) What are the five informative strategies?

(4) How do you plan for an informative speech?

Unit 8  Giving Informative Speeches

# Final Speech Topic

## The Rhetorical Situation

*In 2021, China has achieved Sustainable Development Goal 1 "No Poverty", almost 10 years ahead. The pictures in Activity 8.2 show how people in China have been engaged in fighting against poverty. Imagine you were a university student representative and received the invitation to introduce China's ways of eradicating extreme poverty at the Economic and Social Council Youth Forum, to a group of 35 university attendees from East Asian countries.*

## Step 1

*Read the report[1] about Sustainable Development Goal 1 "No Poverty", and discuss the following questions with your partner.*

(1) What is Goal 1?

(2) What is extreme poverty?

(3) Why is this goal important?

(4) What are the problems identified in this goal?

(5) What can be done to achieve this goal?

 END POVERTY IN ALL ITS FORMS EVERYWHERE

## 1. What Is Goal 1?

It is to end poverty in all its forms everywhere by 2030.

---

1 The United Nations. 2020. Goal 1: No poverty. *The United Nations*. Retrieved May 20, 2022, from The United Nations website.

## 2. What Is Extreme Poverty?

- Extreme poverty often refers to earning less than $1.9 per day[1].
- Extreme poverty is also the denial of basic freedom and human dignity because people in extreme poverty often face discrimination, marginalization or exclusion, and lack the skills, tools and resources to cope with economic setbacks, natural disasters or illnesses.

## 3. Why Is It Important?

People living in extreme poverty are those who are struggling to fulfill the most basic needs like health, education, and access to water, sanitation, etc. The COVID-19 pandemic has made the situation even worse, with tens of millions of people in risk of being pushed back into extreme poverty.

Developing countries will face a devastating social and economic crisis, with the pandemic pushing millions of workers into unemployment, underemployment and working poverty. Having a job also does not guarantee a decent living. In fact, 7.1 percent of employees and their families worldwide were living in extreme poverty in 2019. Now this number is expected to rise in light of the long-term consequences of the pandemic.

## 4. What Can Be Done?

Governments can help create an enabling environment to generate productive employment and job opportunities for the poor and the marginalized.

Science should lead its role in fighting against poverty. In fact, the contribution of science to end poverty has been significant. For example, it has enabled access to safe drinking water, reduced deaths caused by water-borne diseases, and improved hygiene to reduce health risks related to unsafe drinking water and lack of sanitation.

## Step 2

*You are now about to read a passage[2] introducing how China has successfully managed to end poverty in 2021. Discuss the following question with your partner.*

What did China do to end extreme poverty?

---

1 The World Bank. 2022. Understanding poverty: Overview. *The World Bank*. Retrieved October 21, 2022, from The World Bank website.

2 China Global Television Network. 2021. Targeted poverty relief: China's way to achieve prosperity. *CGTN*. Retrieved March 21, from CGTN website.

Unit 8  Giving Informative Speeches

China officially announced its victory in eradicating absolute poverty on Thursday, February 25, 2021. What has played a key role in reducing the country's poverty is called "targeted poverty alleviation" ( 精准扶贫 ). It is a strategy that designs specific relief policies for different local conditions. The concept was put forward in November 2013 by Chinese President Xi Jinping when he visited Shibadong, a Miao ethnic minority village, nestled in the mountains of central China's Hunan Province.

China explored a number of targeted and scientific alleviation measures. This exploration process requires officials to use their expertise and identify actual impoverished people and the factors that caused their poverty. For example, officials with business savvy were sent to poverty-stricken villages, while officials with specialized industrial knowledge were sent to villages with an industrial base. As a result, each household or even family member has been given a poverty relief plan.

China also targeted different policies to different regions, including developing business, relocating the poor, compensating farmers in ecologically fragile areas, encouraging education and improving social security. Moreover, a list of top 10 poverty alleviation projects was introduced including reducing poverty through e-commerce, tourism, and photovoltaic power generation projects.

The government also motivated businesses, individuals, Non-governmental Organizations (NGOs) and even the military to carry out relief plans. Wealthier provinces were designated at least one less-developed province to provide special guidance and assistance.

With these measurements, China accomplished its poverty alleviation target of the new era in November 2020, despite the unprecedented impacts brought by COVID-19. It has lifted 98.99 million poor rural residents out of poverty under the current poverty line, with 832 impoverished counties and 128,000 poor villages removed from the poverty list, achieving the poverty reduction target of the UN 2030 Agenda for Sustainable Development 10 years ahead of schedule.

Given China's large population, its victory against absolute poverty is also a significant contribution to the global cause of poverty reduction and set a pioneering example for the international community, especially when the raging COVID-19 pandemic is dragging an increasing number of people into poverty across the world.

**Step 3**

*With the notes from your reading and discussion, prepare an informative speech on "How China Has Managed to Eradicate Extreme Poverty" based on the rhetorical situation given in this unit. You can also use your notes from all the activities in this unit to prepare your speech. Be aware of the general goal of your speech being informative.*

# Unit 9
## Giving Persuasive Speeches

# OBJECTIVES

After studying this unit, you should be able to:

(1) Understand what a persuasive speech is, and how it is different from an informative speech.

(2) See why it is difficult to persuade people.

(3) Identify certain ways to make persuasion easier.

(4) Know the Motivation Sequence as an effective way to structure persuasive speeches.

(5) Practice how to structure a persuasive speech.

# Warm Up

## Step 1

## In Pairs

*The ocean is a continuous body of salt water. It covers more than 70% of the Earth's surface. Discuss the following questions about ocean with your partner.*

(1) What three words would you use to describe the ocean?

(2) What can the ocean do for human beings?

Unit 9   Giving Persuasive Speeches

## Step 2

## By Yourself

*Suppose your goal was to convince your class that the ocean is extremely important and needs protection. How will you change your answers to the two questions above?*

## 9.1   What Is a Persuasive Speech?

A persuasive speech is one that aims to alter another person's point of view, to agree with you, or even do something. The general purposes most likely used in a persuasive speech are to:

| 1. Change people's opinions completely. | 2. Make people feel weaker about a topic. |
|---|---|
| **Persuasive Speeches Aim to** | |
| 4. Make people feel stronger about a topic. | 3. Make people do something. |

So whereas an informative speech on $CO_2$ might be one that informs the audience about what carbon release is, a persuasive speech can be one that tries to make the audience:

- believe that $CO_2$ emissions cost the world plenty of money;
- know that $CO_2$ emissions hurt nature and people;
- take action to reduce these emissions.

## 9.2   Why Is It Difficult to Persuade People?

It is difficult to change people's opinions because they are psychologically constrained by their own ideas and beliefs. What makes it difficult to persuade people includes:

| Selective Exposure | • People choose to go to speeches that agree with their own ideas. |
|---|---|

| Selective Attention | • People choose to focus on, follow and take in messages that agree with their own ideas. |

| Selective Perception | • People choose to understand a message according to their own experiences. |

When persuading others, you are basically telling them that what they believe or think is wrong. That is challenging. So, it is important to be realistic in your general purpose. Do you think you can completely change the opinions of other people, or is it better to give them some doubts?

## 9.3  How to Reduce the Constraints on Persuasive Speeches?

It seems that persuading is very difficult, but there are still some ways to make it easier. The following methods can help you reduce the constraints on persuasive speeches.

(1) Be clear on your arguments and reduce any misunderstanding.

(2) Start with things you and your audience agree with.

(3) Make your persuasion small and specific.

(4) Make sure the topic is applied to your audience.

(5) Establish credibility for you and your audience.

(6) Expose inconsistencies in the audience's compartmentalization.

(7) Put yourself in the shoes of the audience and consider how they might interpret your speech.

(8) Offer solutions that are doable for the audience.

## Activity 9.1  Reducing Constraints

### By Yourself

*Below is an excerpt from a speech titled "The Fastest Way to Slow Down Climate Change*

Unit 9　Giving Persuasive Speeches

Now"[1]. The speaker is persuading the audience to reduce their use of methane. The persuasion is difficult because methane is a natural gas widely used in daily life. Read the excerpt and identify the methods the speaker uses to reduce constraints on her speech. Write down the numbers of the sentences responding to the methods and then compare your notes with your partner.

| Speech | Identifying Methods |
|---|---|
| (1) Today, I want to show you how big of a dent we are making in our natural resources, and what steps we should take next. (2) Let's say you want to throw away one plastic water bottle. Okay, no big deal. It's just one bottle right? Well, Charleston is a peninsula, meaning that we are entirely surrounded by the ocean. (3) According to Hannah Ellsbury in her article "The Problem with Plastic", for every six water bottles we use, only one makes it to the recycling bin. The rest are sent to landfills. Or, even worse, they end up as trash on the land and in rivers, lakes, and the ocean. That means that, on average, all of us in this room cumulatively throw away or litter 6,100 water bottles a year. Now, let's say that about 1/4 of these end up in our beautiful Charleston harbor. That's about 1,525 bottles just floating around outside of Charleston in a year, and that's strictly from our first year seminar class alone. (4) Pollutants found in the plastic in disposable water bottles deteriorate and leach into the water leaving potential carcinogens in the water we drink daily. Now if all 1,525 water bottles in our harbor are deteriorating, that means our fresh seafood at Hyman's might be slightly infested with pollutants. | Which methods in the following are used in the speech?<br><br>_____ (a) Be clear on your arguments and what you want the audience to do.<br><br>_____ (b) Start with things you agree with the audience about.<br><br>_____ (c) Make small persuasions.<br><br>_____ (d) Make the speech topic applied to the listeners.<br><br>_____ (e) Establish credibility. |

---

1　Ocko, I. 2021. The fastest way to slow down climate change now. *TEDx*. Retrieved May 30, 2022, from TEDx website.

(Continued)

| Speech | Identifying Methods |
|---|---|
| …<br>(5) <u>There is no reason plastic cups should still be sold on campus, and I propose a small fee should be charged for every purchase involving plastic.</u><br><br>Now I'm hoping that you're interested in doing something to help cut down on the pollutants entering, not only your body, but millions of aquatic sea creatures as well. You know the harmful effects of plastic on our environment and you know the dent we put in our planet in the production of these goods. (6) <u>We should all make an effort to use reusable water bottles, however, if we must, to recycle our plastic waste.</u> We must put an end to the era of plastic so this little guy can swim freely, but only our generation can do so. | _____ (f) Expose inconsistencies in the audience's compartmentalization.<br><br>_____ (g) Put yourself in the shoes of the audience.<br><br>_____ (h) Offer solutions that are doable for each person. |

## 9.4 How to Structure a Persuasive Speech?

Earlier, you have learnt what general purposes can be used in a persuasive speech. Now, let's discuss how to structure a persuasive speech to meet each purpose. For each general purpose, there is a list of methods provided. Take a look at persuasive strategies, and consider how you can apply them. It may be helpful to consider persuasion as chess playing. Most of the time when you want to change another person's opinion, it is all about the strategies or steps you decide to take.

### 1. To Completely Change the Audience's Opinion on Something, You Can:

- Start by showing how the audience's opinion and your opinion can live together, but slowly move to where they are in conflict. This can build a connection with your audience before you completely change to why they are wrong.
- Explain why the arguments of the audience are wrong, and attack their opinion. As you can imagine, this may cause the audience to deny your ideas but it can be quick.

- Focus on arguing why you are right. It is more positive than attacking the audience's opinion, and can convince them.
- Make small attempts to do small changes. You can admit that you cannot change their opinion completely today, but try to make tiny changes and then try again later.
- You can use testimony of somebody who used to agree with the audience, but now doesn't. This can be a powerful way to show them that it is possible to change.

## 2. To Make the Audience Feel Weaker About a Topic, You Can:

- Directly challenge the audience's arguments.
- Identify what things may limit the audience's commitment to the topic, and then discuss these things. This means to look for the weakest points in their opinion and discuss them.
- Rebuild your argument that has been attacked by the audience. So instead of directly challenging them, you can "rebuild" the topic by starting with redefining the topic that fits you. Your rebuilding/redefining would make it more natural to put forward your arguments, and also make it easier for the audience to trust you and hear your reasoning.

## 3. To Make the Audience Feel Stronger About a Topic, You Can:

- Remind the audience of its importance.
- Convince the audience that the issue is so important that they need to do something.
- Make the response to the issue more urgent.

## 4. To Make the Audience Do Something, Our Advice Is to:

- Be clear on what you want the audience to do so that they do not misunderstand you.
- Make the action simple.

Apart from the above strategies, there are some general tips for giving persuasive speeches:

(1) Use appropriate supporting information for your audience and rhetorical situation (see Unit 4).

(2) Choose an appropriate organizational pattern. Cause and effect, problem and solution, compare and contrast, and residue are the most common ways, but you can certainly mix and match them. A speech that offers a cause, effect and solution is a mix, and can be very powerful (see Unit 5).

(3) Build credibility in your introduction so that the audience have a reason to trust your arguments (see Unit 6).

(4) Combine informative structures with persuasive ones. For example, a persuasive speech can involve the chronological structure when you describe a policy (see Unit 8).

(5) Use your voice, body and visual aids to help convince different kinds of audience (see Unit 10).

## 9.5 Exemplifying Structuring Persuasive Speeches: the Motivation Sequence

The Motivation Sequence is one common way to structure a persuasive speech. In this structure, the speech would:

- Get the attention of the audience.
- Describe the need for change.
- Provide a solution.
- Show what the world would look like by visualizing it.
- Ask the audience to take action.

The Motivation Sequence is most commonly used in advertisement. The following is an example of a hypothetical advertisement about yogurt:

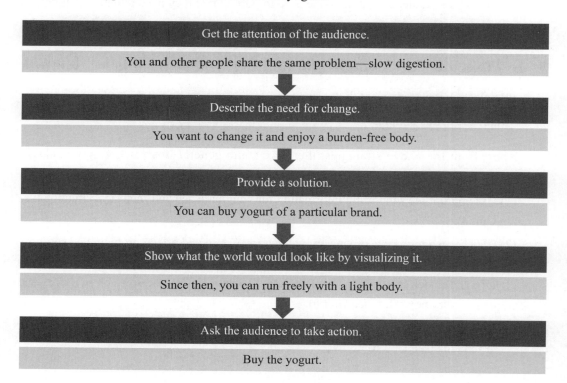

Unit 9  Giving Persuasive Speeches

## Activity 9.2  Structuring a Persuasive Speech

*Now, you will go through the process of making a persuasive speech with the following scenario. The complete description of the rhetorical situation can be found at the end of this unit. Here, you can only focus on the application of the persuasive strategies.*

You are an actor of ActNow, the UN campaign for individual actions that are dedicated to climate action and sustainability. You want to persuade your college mates to act for the United Nations Sustainable Development Goal 14 "Life Below Water" and take eco-friendly action to protect the ocean. You want to focus on persuading your audience that they should use less food delivery service because packages of food delivery are not eco-friendly.

| Your Topic | To encourage university students to take eco-friendly action by using less food delivery service. |
|---|---|
| Your General Purposes | • To make people feel weaker about something.<br>• To make people do something. |
| Your Specific Purposes | • To let people become more aware that food delivery service is not so good compared with university canteens.<br>• To let people reduce their use of plastic packaging. |
| Your Audience | Your college mates who have been using lots of food delivery services. |

### Step 1  Analyzing the Constraints

In Pairs

*During your research, you have found that food delivery can cause a lot of plastic waste. Brainstorm what may stop college students from being convinced by you to give up food delivery service with your partner.*

| The Constraints You May Encounter | (1) _____<br>(2) _____<br>(3) _____ |
|---|---|

### Step 2  Choosing Persuasive Strategies

In Pairs

*Choose three strategies below that may help you reduce the constraints that you've listed above. Write down your plan as to what to do to make your speech more persuasive.*

| Persuasive Strategies | Your Plan |
|---|---|
| • Be clear on your arguments and reduce any misunderstanding.<br>• Start with things you and your audience agree with.<br>• Make your persuasion small and specific.<br>• Make sure the topic is applied to your audience.<br>• Establish credibility for you and your audience.<br>• Expose inconsistencies in the audience's compartmentalization.<br>• Put yourself in the shoes of the audience and consider how they might interpret your speech.<br>• Offer solutions that are doable for the audience. | |

## Step 3  Outlining Your Speech

# In Pairs

*Use the three constraints from Step 1, and outline the body of your speech. Complete the following table with your partner.*

| General Purpose | To make college students do something. |
|---|---|
| Specific Purpose | To make college students use less food delivery service. |
| Constraint 1 | |
| How You Will Tackle Constraint 1 | |
| Supporting Information 1 | |
| Constraint 2 | |
| How You Will Tackle Constraint 2 | |
| Supporting Information 2 | |

# Unit 9  Giving Persuasive Speeches

(Continued)

| | |
|---|---|
| **Constraint 3** | |
| **How You Will Tackle Constraint 3** | |
| **Supporting Information 3** | |

## Step 4  Comparing and Evaluating

## In Groups

*Join up with a neighboring pair to form a small group of four. Explain your persuasion plan to the other pair and invite them to give you feedback on the effect of persuasion. Use the table below to guide your feedback.*

(1) After knowing your plan, would they like to hear more about your speech?
☐ Yes
☐ No
☐ Not sure

Because _____
_____

(2) After hearing your plan, will they give up using food delivery service?
☐ Yes
☐ No
☐ Not sure

Because _____
_____

(3) What else would they prefer to be included in your persuasion plan?
_____
_____
_____
_____

## 9.6 Final Questions

(1) What is a persuasive speech? How is it different from an informative speech?

(2) Why is it particularly difficult to persuade people? What are constraining people from believing an opinion different from their own?

(3) How do you make persuasion easier in public speaking?

(4) What is the Motivation Sequence?

# Final Speech Topic

### The Rhetorical Situation

*You are an actor of ActNow, the UN campaign for individual actions that are dedicated to climate action and sustainability. You want to persuade your college mates to act for the United Nations Sustainable Development Goal 14 "Life Below Water" and take eco-friendly action. You want to focus on persuading your audience that they should use less food delivery service because packages of food delivery are not eco-friendly to the ocean.*

### Step 1

*Read the report[1] about Sustainable Development Goal 14 "Life Below Water", and discuss the following questions with your partner.*

(1) What is addressed in Goal 14?

(2) Why is this goal important?

(3) What are the problems identified in this goal?

(4) What can be done to achieve this goal?

---

1 The United Nations. 2020. Goal 14: Life below water. *The United Nations*. Retrieved June 11, 2022, from The United Nations website.

Unit 9   Giving Persuasive Speeches

 **CONSERVE AND SUSTAINABLY USE THE OCEANS, SEA AND MARINE RESOURCES FOR SUSTAINABLE DEVELOPMENT**

## 1. What Is Goal 14?

It is to conserve and sustainably use the world's oceans, sea and marine resources.

## 2. Why Is It Important?

Oceans are our planet's life support and regulate the global climate system. They are the world's largest ecosystem, home to nearly a million known species and containing vast untapped potential for scientific discovery. Oceans and fisheries continue to support the global population's economic, social and environmental needs.

Despite the critical importance of conserving oceans, decades of irresponsible exploitation has led to an alarming level of degradation. Current efforts to protect key marine environments and small-scale fisheries, and to invest in ocean science are not yet meeting the urgent need to safeguard this vast but fragile resource.

## 3. What Are the Problems?

The oceans absorb around 23 percent of annual $CO_2$ emissions generated by human activity and help mitigate the impacts of climate change. The oceans also absorb more than 90 percent of the excess heat in the climate system. Increasing levels of rubbish in the world's oceans are having a major environmental and economic impact. Every year, about 5 million to 12 million metric tons of plastic enters the ocean, costing roughly $13 billion per year—including clean-up costs and financial losses in fisheries and other industries. About 89 percent of plastic litter found on the ocean floor are single-use items like plastic bags.

## 4. What Can Be Done?

On a local level, people should make ocean-friendly choices when buying products or eating food derived from oceans and consume only what they need. Selecting certified products is a good place to start. They should eliminate plastic usage as much as possible and organize beach clean-ups. Most importantly, they should spread the message about how important marine life is and why they need to protect it.

## Step 2

*You are now about to read a news article[1] on the 2022 United Nations Ocean Conference. Discuss the following questions with your partner.*

(1) What is the theme of this year's Ocean Conference?

(2) What is Blue Partnerships?

(3) What action has China taken to follow Blue Partnerships?

The 2022 United Nations Ocean Conference was held from June 27 to July 2 in Lisbon, the Portuguese capital. As a critical opportunity to make progress towards achieving Sustainable Development Goal 14, it has aroused worldwide attention and expectation.

While the overall theme of the conference was "Scaling Up Ocean Action Based on Science and Innovation for the Implementation of Goal 14: Stocktaking, Partnerships and Solutions", the Chinese delegation has highlighted "Blue Partnerships" as one of the important measures China is taking in response to the UN 2030 Agenda goal.

Blue Partnerships was one of the initiatives China proposed at the 2017 UN Ocean Conference, together with two other initiatives, "Vigorously Developing a Blue Economy" and "Promoting a Marine Ecological Civilization". The Blue Partnerships Principles reflect China's determination and ambition to actively participate in and lead the global ocean sustainable development and protection.

As to the common actions under the Blue Partnerships, several measures have been recommended such as science and technology innovation, implementation of ecosystem-based integrated ocean management, promotion of solutions and enhancing capacity building. China has also participated in international cooperation on marine plastic pollution, regulating global transport of waste and pollutants, ocean monitoring, as well as building the capacity of coastal and island countries on marine spatial planning and development of the blue economy.

---

1 Xie, X. & Yeung, C. 2022. Sea change. *China Daily*. Retrieved July 5, 2022, from China Daily website.

Unit 9　Giving Persuasive Speeches

## Step 3

*With the notes from your reading and discussion, prepare a speech based on the rhetorical situation given in this unit. Draft the body of your speech persuading your college mates to use less food delivery service. You can adopt your draft on what you have done in Activity 9.2 and the techniques you've learnt in this unit.*

# Unit 10

# Performing Speeches

# OBJECTIVES

After studying this unit, you should be able to:

(1) Know different ways of using notes, and the pros and cons of each method.

(2) Identify ways to make your presentation style more interesting.

(3) Use voice, body and visual aids to give an interesting speech.

# Warm Up

### Step 1

### By Yourself

*List six emotions. Try to be creative.*

(1) _____

(2) _____

(3) _____

(4) _____

(5) _____

(6) _____

Unit 10　Performing Speeches

## Step 2

## In Pairs

*Each student chooses two emotions. Take turns reading the sentences in the table below with each emotion, and then read them again with no emotion. Then share your thoughts with your partner by considering the following questions.*

(1) Which emotion made the reading the most interesting to listen to? Why?

(2) Which emotion made the reading the least interesting to listen to? Why?

(3) Did each emotion change the meaning of the sentences? How?

(4) How did you feel, as a speaker and listener respectively, when using no emotion? Why?

| |
|---|
| • I am from the south. |
| • Are you using your phone? |
| • I had a haircut. |
| • My friend cooked for me last night. |

## 10.1　How to Use Notes During Speaking?

There are many ways of using notes. For example:

(1) No notes at all.

(2) Reading notes word for word.

(3) Memorizing notes.

(4) Using flashcards.

(5) Using PowerPoint.

The following are the pros and cons of each method.

| No Notes at All ||
|---|---|
| Pros | Cons |
| • It allows you to be flexible.<br>• You don't need to prepare every word.<br>• You can focus more on interacting with the audience, using your voice and moving around. | • It can be more difficult to remember the content.<br>• You might become afraid of not preparing every word.<br>• If you are not confident in yourself, it might be difficult. |

| Reading Notes Word for Word | |
|---|---|
| **Pros** | **Cons** |
| • You won't forget anything.<br>• It's helpful when you don't have much time to prepare.<br>• It's helpful when you are not confident in delivering the speech. | • It tends to make a very boring speech.<br>• You can't have eye contacts with the audience so you don't know how they react.<br>• Your voice will be boring.<br>• You may just end up standing in one spot. |

| Memorizing Notes | |
|---|---|
| **Pros** | **Cons** |
| • You can remember all your ideas.<br>• It helps if you're not confident. | • Your audience get bored as they know you are memorizing.<br>• You don't act naturally.<br>• You focus too much on trying to remember the words, while forgetting everything else like voice, body language, etc.<br>• You may not know what to do if you forget a word. |

| Using Flashcards | |
|---|---|
| **Pros** | **Cons** |
| • Using small cards with your key points on them helps you remember all the main ideas.<br>• It helps you speak naturally. | • You may forget the sentences. |

| Using PowerPoint | |
|---|---|
| **Pros** | **Cons** |
| • You already have the PowerPoint slides so it may not take any extra work.<br>• Good PowerPoint slides are clear in content and provide you with everything you need.<br>• It helps you speak naturally and be flexible. | • It may cause you to spend too much time looking at the computer or the projected PowerPoint slides.<br>• You may be tempted to put too much writing on the PowerPoint slides and just read them out.<br>• You won't have every word planned. |

Unit 10  Performing Speeches

By looking at the imbalance between the pros and cons of each method, you may already have a clear picture about how to use the methods to deliver a speech.

## Activity 10.1  Using Notes

### In Groups

*1) You are going to prepare and deliver a 30-second self-introduction according to the following information.*

  (1) **Person 1:** Write down every word, and read it to the other two listeners.

  (2) **Person 2:** Write down and memorize every word, and speak to the other two listeners.

  (3) **Person 3:** Make a flashcard with only 10 words on it, and speak to the other two listeners.

*2) After finishing, talk about your experiences as a speaker and listener with the following questions.*

  (1) Which one was easier to remember? Why?

  (2) Which one allowed you more freedom to change things? Why?

  (3) Which one was easier to change your voice to make it more interesting? Why?

  (4) Which one was better to listen to? Why?

## 10.2  How to Use Voice to Make Your Presentation More Interesting?

A speech can be more interesting when you use a good presentation style. How can you make your presentation style more interesting? You can do it by:

- using your voice in various ways.
- using unique movement and body language.
- being creative in your visuals.

Using your voice in a variety of ways can make your speeches more interesting and get the audience to really understand what you want them to do. How can you use your voice to make your speech more attractive? The following is a list of elements that you need to focus on:

**Volume**
- How loud you speak.
- Use the microphone if you are worried that the audience can't hear you.

**Emotion**
- Use feelings when speaking.
- It helps make your speech interesting and aids your audience in knowing how to feel what you are talking about.

**Pausing**
- Stop for a period of time.
- It can give your audience time to think about what you are saying, or to see that you have said something very important.

**Pitch**
- How high or low you speak.
- Varying pitch can keep your audience interested, or emphasize key words, or to show if something is a question or statement.

**Speed**
- How fast you speak.
- Speaking slower is useful to help people understand key points or complex ideas.
- Speaking faster is useful to build drama.

Unit 10   Performing Speeches

# Activity 10.2   Intonation Practice

## Step 1

## By Yourself

***Read aloud the following passage and use your phone to record the first reading.***

> When you get to school, things are pushed at you: knowledge, exams, systems, and timetables. If you want to attract people like Juan who could, for instance, wear jewelry and ride motorbikes into education, having a compulsory curriculum doesn't really make sense. You need to pull him. And so education needs to work by pull, not push. So you need education to be relevant and help people make a living there and then. And you also need to make it intrinsically interesting.

## Step 2

## By Yourself

***Now, follow the instructions below and mark the text with voice markers. Read it again with the indications from your voice markers and record it again with your phone.***

(1) Look for any parts of the text that can be used with emotions, and underline them with a squiggly line "〰". Also, make a note of the emotion you will use when presenting.

(2) Look for key words in each sentence, and circle "◯" them out. These key words will be spoken at a higher pitch.

(3) Look for points in each sentence where you can pause and take a breath. A comma ",", or a full stop "." are obvious ones, but long sentences can have a break in the middle of them. Put a pause "/" every time you can have a small break.

(4) Look for moments of drama or excitement. Put brackets "( )" around the beginning and the end of these parts. These parts will be spoken quicker, while the rest of the text will be spoken slower.

(5) Look for parts that might be confusing for the audience. Use square brackets "[ ]" here. These parts need a slower speech, and also a pause to give people a chance to process the information.

**Step 3**

## In Pairs

*Now, it's time for a comparison. Play the two recordings to your partner. Which one does your partner like more? Why?*

## 10.3 How to Use Your Body to Make Your Presentation More Interesting?

It can be incredibly boring to watch a speech where the speaker just stands at the computer, looking at the screen and ignoring the audience. While engaging your body into the speech, you can encourage more people to listen to you. Here are some methods to engage your body during speaking:

### 1. Your Body

If you are telling a story, use your body to do the actions, or to show how big something is, or the other ways of using gestures. Just be careful of using too much, or unnatural body language.

### 2. Facial Expressions

You can use your face to show emotions and to get people interested in what you are talking about.

### 3. The Place Where You Stand

Different rhetorical situations will have different expectations. For example, a speech to a forum of the United Nations will have a special podium for you to stand at, and to move away from this can be dangerous. If you have more freedom, then please get away from the computer and stand somewhere that is more interactive with the audience.

### 4. Eye Contact

Looking at your audience can make them feel like you are talking to them. Eye contact shows confidence, and this confidence can help make good speeches.

## 5. Your Posture

This means how you stand or sit. Remember to make yourself look professional.

## 6. Your Physical Appearance

This means your hairstyle, clothing, or anything else related to your appearance. People will judge you based on how you look.

## Activity 10.3   Acting During Speaking

### Step 1

### In Groups

*Sit in a circle and take some time to think about what you did last weekend. You are going to describe this weekend for one minute to the other members of your group. While describing your weekend, stand up and do as follows.*

> **Person 1:** Move hands a lot to help people understand the key points.
>
> **Person 2:** Walk around the group.
>
> **Person 3:** Look at each person one by one when speaking.
>
> **Person 4:** Use facial expressions.
>
> **Person 5:** Stand still, don't use hands or facial expressions, and look down.

### Step 2

### In Groups

*After finishing, discuss the following questions within the group.*

> (1) Which speaker was the most interesting? Why?
>
> (2) What did you think of the last speaker? Why?
>
> (3) How did the use of the body affect the speech?

## 10.4 How to Use Visuals to Make Your Presentation More Interesting?

There is no need for you to always use visual aids. It has to depend on the rhetorical situation. Here are some issues for you to consider when choosing a visual aid for your speech.

### 1. Why Should You Use Visual Aids?

- They can make your speeches more interesting.
- They can help the audience understand and remember your points.
- They can be more convincing.
- They can make a speech more professional.

### 2. What Kinds of Visual Aids Can You Use?

- Handouts

These are the things you give to the audience to look at during the speech. They are great as they allow the audience to look at them in their own time and be able to take them home. However, be aware that handouts can take the attention away from you. So use them carefully.

- People

You can get somebody to come with you to act things out to make a message clearer. Be careful of things like role plays, as they can make a speech look unprofessional.

- Objects

Imagine a speech on Chinese painting. It may be really interesting to bring some copies of famous Chinese paintings, some types of paint commonly used and the paint brushes.

- Audio and videos

Using recorded sounds and videos can enhance your points. There are so many things you can do, but do not allow the video and audio to replace you.

### 3. More on PowerPoint

PowerPoint is visual, so do not put your entire speech on it. You also want your audience to focus on you, rather than the computer screen. You can use PowerPoint for:

- key words;
- charts;

Unit 10   Performing Speeches

- graphs;
- visual representation;
- videos and sounds.

It is recommended to keep a few (no more than three) sentences on a slide, and some key words for each sentence. Also, the general rule is about one minute for presenting each PowerPoint slide. If you find yourself going slower, it indicates that you have more information on the slide.

## Activity 10.4   Finding Mistakes

## In Pairs

*1) Discuss the following questions with your partner.*

(1) What problems can you see on the PowerPoint slide below?

(2) What changes will you make to improve it?

### HOW TO USE POWERPOINT

**When preparing your PowerPoint:**

- First, use a design that is appropriate for the situation.
- Second, look at the colors and color combinations. Building on the idea of colors, you can use color to create moods or to make things stand out.
- Third, make sure the font style is readable, and the font size is big enough for people at the back to see.
- Fourth, make sure you don't put too much or too little on each slide.
- Fifth, make sure the charts, graphs and pictures are big enough and easy to follow.
- Sixth, you can use animations.

*2) Now, go back to your speech about last weekend in Activity 10.3. Imagine you would give this speech to your class, but your teacher has banned PowerPoint. You have to use two other forms of visual aids. What will you choose? Why? Share your answers with your partner.*

## 10.5　Final Questions

(1) What are the different ways of using notes? What are the pros and cons of each method?

(2) Why do you need to use your voice, body language and visual aids while speaking?

(3) What are some alternatives to visual aids?

(4) How can you use your voice, body language and visual aids while speaking?

# Final Speech Topic

> ### The Rhetorical Situation
>
> *You are a news reporter who will provide a one minute news report on the United Nations Alliance of Civilization Young Peacebuilder, focusing on:*
>
> *(1) Describing Sustainable Development Goal 17 "Partnerships for the Goals" as the background framework.*
>
> *(2) Introducing China's understanding of a peaceful and harmonious humanity.*
>
> *(3) Issues people are facing in today's world.*
>
> *(4) Calling on all youth to join hand in hand in peace building.*

### Step 1

*Read the report[1] about Sustainable Development Goal 17 "Partnerships for the Goals", and discuss the following questions with your partner.*

(1) What is addressed in Goal 17?

(2) Why is this goal important?

(3) What can be done to achieve this goal?

---

1　The United Nations. 2020. Goal 17: Global partnership. *The United Nations*. Retrieved April 21, 2022, from The United Nations website.

# Unit 10  Performing Speeches

**STRENGTHEN THE MEANS OF IMPLEMENTATION AND REVITALIZE THE GLOBAL PARTNERSHIP FOR SUSTAINABLE DEVELOPMENT**

## 1. What Is Goal 17?

It is to revitalize the global partnership for sustainable development.

## 2. Why Is It Important?

In the post-pandemic era, global partnerships are more important than ever if people are to solve world's problems. They must be united. Governments, civil society, scientists, academia and private sectors need to come together. Goal 17 calls for action by all countries, both developed and developing, to ensure no one is left behind. People are all in this together.

### Step 2

*You are about to read "Work Together to Build a Community of Shared Future for Mankind" in Appendix. It is President Xi's keynote speech at the United Nations Office in Geneva, Switzerland, on January 18, 2017. Discuss the following questions with your partner.*

(1) Why should people build a community of shared future for mankind?

(2) What is China's standpoint on the issue?

(3) On what principle can people build a harmonious human community?

### Step 3

*Present your news report based on the rhetorical situation given in this unit. Before your presentation, take a look through questions below and consider how you can make your report more interesting and easy to understand. This report can be recorded with the help of a camera or phone.*

(1) How will you use notes?

- Read
- Memorize
- Use flashcards
- Remember key points

(2) Which parts of your news report will use these notes?

- Emotion
- Pause
- Pitch
- Speed

(3) How will you use your body?

- Body language
- Facial expressions
- The place where you stand
- Eye contact
- Posture
- Appearance

(4) How will you use visual aids?

- Handouts
- People
- Objects
- Posters
- Flip charts
- Audio
- Video
- PowerPoint

# Appendix

## Work Together to Build a Community of Shared Future for Mankind[1]

Your Excellency Mr. Peter Thomson, President of the 71st Session of the UN General Assembly, Your Excellency Mr. António Guterres, UN Secretary-General, Your Excellency Mr. Michael Møller, Director-General of the UN Office at Geneva, ladies and gentlemen, friends.

As a new year begins, everything takes on a new look, and it gives me great pleasure to visit the United Nations Office at Geneva and discuss with you the building of a community of shared future for mankind, which is the call of our time.

I just attended the World Economic Forum Annual Meeting. In Davos, many speakers pointed out in their speeches that today's world is full of uncertainties and that people long for a bright future but are bewildered about what will come. What has happened to the world and how should we respond? The whole world is reflecting on this question, and it is also very much on my mind.

I believe that to answer this question, we need to get clear about a fundamental issue: Where did we come from? Where are we now? And where are we going?

Over the past century and more, mankind has gone through bloody hot wars and the chilling "Cold War", but also achieved remarkable development and huge progress. In the first half of last century, mankind suffered the scourges of two world wars, and the people yearned for the end of war and the advent of peace. In the 1950s and 1960s, people in colonies awakened and fought to shake off shackles and achieve independence. Since the end of the "Cold War", people have pursued a shared aspiration, namely, to expand cooperation and promote common development.

---

1 Xi, J. P. 2017. Work together to build a community of shared future for mankind. *Xinhua*. Retrieved June 2, 2022, from Xinhua website.

Peace and development: This has been the aspiration held dear by mankind over the past century. However, the goal to achieve peace and development is far from being met. We need to respond to the people's call, take up the baton of history and forge ahead on the marathon track toward peace and development.

Mankind is in an era of major development as well as profound transformation and change. The trend toward multi-polarity and economic globalization is surging. IT application in social development and cultural diversity are making continued progress. A new round of scientific and industrial revolution is in the making. Interconnection and interdependence between countries are crucial for human survival. The forces for peace far outweigh factors causing war, and the trend of our times toward peace, development, cooperation and win-win outcomes has gained stronger momentum.

On the other hand, mankind is also in an era of numerous challenges and increasing risks. Global growth is sluggish, the impact of the financial crisis lingers on and the development gap is widening. Armed conflicts occur from time to time, "Cold War" mentality and power politics still exist and non-conventional security threats, particularly terrorism, refugee crisis, major communicable diseases and climate change, are spreading.

There is only one Earth in the universe and we mankind have only one homeland. Stephen Hawking has raised the proposition about "parallel universe", hoping to find another place in the universe where mankind could live. We do not know when his wish will come true. Until today, Earth is still the only home to mankind, so to care for and cherish it is the only option for us mankind. There is a Latin motto inscribed in the dome of the Federal Palace of Switzerland which says "Unus pro omnibus, omnes pro uno" (One for all, and all for one). We should not only think about our own generation, but also take responsibility for future ones.

Ladies and gentlemen, friends, pass on the torch of peace from generation to generation, sustain development and make civilization flourish: This is what people of all countries long for; it is also the responsibility statesmen of our generation ought to shoulder. And China's proposition is: build a community of shared future for mankind and achieve shared and win-win development.

Vision guides action and direction determines the future. As modern history shows, to establish a fair and equitable international order is the goal mankind has always striven for. From the principles of equality and sovereignty established in the Peace of Westphalia over 360 years ago to international humanitarianism affirmed in the Geneva Convention 150-plus years ago; from the four purposes and seven principles enshrined in the UN Charter more than 70 years ago to the Five Principles of Peaceful Coexistence championed by the Bandung Conference over 60 years ago, many principles have emerged in the evolution of international

# Appendix    Work Together to Build a Community of Shared Future for Mankind

relations and become widely accepted. These principles should guide us in building a community of shared future for mankind.

Sovereign equality is the most important norm governing state-to-state relations over the past centuries and the cardinal principle observed by the United Nations and all other international organizations. The essence of sovereign equality is that the sovereignty and dignity of all countries, whether big or small, strong or weak, rich or poor, must be respected, their internal affairs allow no interference and they have the right to independently choose their social system and development path. In organizations such as the United Nations, World Trade Organization, World Health Organization, World Intellectual Property Organization, World Meteorological Organization, International Telecommunication Union, Universal Postal Union, International Organization for Migration and International Labor Organization, countries have an equal voice in decision-making, constituting an important force for improving global governance. In a new era, we should uphold sovereign equality and work for equality in right, opportunity and rules for all countries.

Geneva witnessed the adoption of the Final Declaration on the Problem of Restoring Peace in Indo-China, the first summit meeting for reconciliation between the two blocs during the "Cold War" and the dialog and negotiations on hotspot issues like the Iranian nuclear issue and the Syrian issue. What we can learn from both past and present is that dialog and consultation is an effective way to bridge differences and political negotiation is the fundamental solution to end conflicts. When we have sincere wish, goodwill and political wisdom, no conflict is too big to settle and no ice is too thick to break.

An ancient Chinese philosopher said, "Law is the very foundation of governance." Here in Geneva, countries, on the basis of the UN Charter, concluded a number of international conventions and legal documents on political security, trade, development, social issues, human rights, science and technology, health, labor, intellectual property, culture and sports. The relevance of law lies in its enforcement. It is thus incumbent on all countries to uphold the authority of the international rule of law, exercise their rights in accordance with law and fulfill their obligations in good faith. The relevance of law also lies in fairness and justice. All countries and international judicial institutions should ensure equal and uniform application of international law and reject double standards and the practice of applying international law in a selective way, thus ensuring genuine equality and justice in the world.

"The ocean is vast because it admits all rivers." Openness and inclusiveness have made Geneva a center of multilateral diplomacy. We should advance democracy in international relations and reject dominance by just one or several countries. All countries should jointly shape the future of the world, write international rules, manage global affairs and ensure that development outcomes are shared by all.

In 1862, in his book *Un Souvenir de Solférino*, Henry Dunant pondered the question of whether it is possible to set up humanitarian organizations and conclude humanitarian conventions. The answer came one year later with the founding of the International Committee of the Red Cross. Over the past 150-plus years, the Red Cross has become a symbol and a banner. In the face of frequent humanitarian crises, we should champion the spirit of humanity, compassion and dedication and give love and hope to the innocent people caught in dire situations. We should uphold the basic principles of neutrality, impartiality and independence, refrain from politicizing humanitarian issues and ensure non-militarization of humanitarian assistance.

Ladies and gentlemen, friends, great visions can be realized only through actions. Actions hold the key to building a community of shared future for mankind. To achieve this goal, the international community should promote partnership, security, growth, inter-civilization exchanges and the building of a sound ecosystem.

**—We should stay committed to building a world of lasting peace through dialog and consultation.** When countries enjoy peace, so will the world; when countries fight, the world suffers. From the Peloponnesian War in the fifth century BC to the two world wars and the "Cold War" that lasted more than four decades, we have drawn painful and profound lessons. "History, if not forgotten, can serve as a guide for the future." By establishing the United Nations, those before us won more than 70 years of relative peace for the world. What we need to do is to improve the mechanisms and means to more effectively resolve disputes, reduce tension and put an end to wars and conflicts.

The Swiss writer and Nobel laureate Hermann Hesse stressed the importance of serving "not war and destruction but peace and reconciliation". Countries should foster partnerships based on dialog, non-confrontation and non-alliance. Major powers should respect each other's core interests and major concerns, keep their differences under control and build a new model of relations featuring non-conflict, non-confrontation, mutual respect and win-win cooperation. As long as we maintain communication and treat each other with sincerity, the "Thucydides trap" can be avoided. Big countries should treat smaller ones as equals instead of acting as a hegemon imposing their will on others. No country should open the Pandora's box by willfully waging wars or undermining the international rule of law. Nuclear weapons, the Sword of Damocles that hangs over mankind, should be completely prohibited and thoroughly destroyed over time to make the world free of nuclear weapons. Guided by the principle of peace, sovereignty, inclusiveness and shared governance, we should turn the deep sea, the polar regions, the outer space and the Internet into new frontiers for cooperation rather than a wrestling ground for competition.

**—We should build a world of common security for all through joint efforts.** No

# Appendix  Work Together to Build a Community of Shared Future for Mankind

country in the world can enjoy absolute security. A country cannot have security while others are in turmoil, as threats facing other countries may haunt itself also. When neighbors are in trouble, instead of tightening his own fences, one should extend a helping hand to them. As a saying goes, "United we stand, divided we fall." All countries should pursue common, comprehensive, cooperative and sustainable security.

Terrorist attacks that have occurred in Europe, North Africa and the Middle East in recent years once again demonstrate that terrorism is the common enemy of mankind. Fighting terrorism is the shared responsibility of all countries. In fighting terror, we should not just treat the symptoms, but remove its root causes. We should enhance coordination and build a global united front against terrorism so as to create an umbrella of security for people around the world. The number of refugees has hit a record high since the end of the Second World War. While tackling the crisis, we should also get to its roots. Why would anyone want to be displaced if they have a home to return to? UNHCR and the International Organization for Migration should act as the coordinator to mobilize the whole world to respond effectively to the refugee crisis. China has decided to provide an additional 200 million yuan of humanitarian assistance for refugees and the displaced of Syria. As terrorism and refugee crises are closely linked to geopolitical conflicts, resolving conflicts provides the fundamental solution to such problems. Parties directly involved should return to the negotiating table, and other parties should work to facilitate talks for peace, and we should all respect the role the UN plays as the main channel for mediation. Pandemic diseases such as bird flu, Ebola and Zika have sounded the alarm for international health security. The WHO should play a leadership role in strengthening epidemic monitoring and sharing of information, practices and technologies. The international community should step up support and assistance for public health in African countries and other developing countries.

**—We should build a world of common prosperity through win-win cooperation.** Development is the top priority for all countries. Instead of beggaring thy neighbor, countries should stick together like passengers in the same boat. All countries, the main economies in particular, should strengthen macro policy coordination, pursue both current and long-term interests and focus on resolving deep-seated problems. We should seize the historic opportunity presented by the new round of scientific and technological revolution and industrial transformation, shift growth models, drive growth through innovation and further unleash social productivity and social creativity. We should uphold WTO rules, support an open, transparent, inclusive and nondiscriminatory multilateral trading regime and build an open world economy. Trade protectionism and self-isolation will benefit no one.

Economic globalization, a surging historical trend, has greatly facilitated trade, investment, flow of people and technological advances. Since the turn of the century, under the auspices of the UN and riding on the waves of economic globalization, the international community has set the Millennium Development Goals and the 2030 Agenda for Sustainable Development. Thanks to these initiatives, 1.1 billion people have been lifted out of poverty, 1.9 billion people now have access to safe drinking water, 3.5 billion people have gained access to the Internet, and the goal has been set to eradicate extreme poverty by 2030. All this demonstrates that economic globalization is moving in the right direction. Of course, challenges such as development disparity, governance dilemma, digital divide and equity deficit still exist. But they are growing pains. We should face these problems and tackle them, instead of taking no action, as we Chinese like to say, one should not stop eating for fear of getting choked.

We should draw inspiration from history. Historians told us long ago that rapid economic development makes social reform necessary; but people tend to support the former while rejecting the latter. Instead of watching in hesitation, we should move forward against all odds. Answers can also be found in reality. The 2008 international financial crisis teaches us that we should strengthen coordination and improve governance so as to ensure sound growth of economic globalization and make it open, inclusive, balanced and beneficial to all. We should both make the cake bigger and share it fairly to ensure justice and equity.

Last September, the G20 Summit in Hangzhou focused on global economic governance and other major issues, adopted the Blueprint on Innovative Growth, put development for the first time in global macro policy framework, and formulated an action plan.

**—We should build an open and inclusive world through exchanges and mutual learning.** Delicious soup is made by combining different ingredients. Diversity of human civilizations not only defines our world, but also drives progress of mankind. There are more than 200 countries and regions, over 2,500 ethnic groups and multiple religions in our world. Different histories, national conditions, ethnic groups and customs give birth to different civilizations and make the world a colorful one. There is no such thing as a superior or inferior civilization, and civilizations are different only in identity and location. Diversity of civilizations should not be a source of global conflict; rather, it should be an engine driving the advance of human civilizations.

Every civilization, with its own appeal and root, is a human treasure. Diverse civilizations should draw on each other to achieve common progress. We should make exchanges among civilizations a source of inspiration for advancing human society and a bond that keeps the world in peace.

**—We should make our world clean and beautiful by pursuing green and low-carbon development.** Man coexists with nature, which means that any harm to nature will eventually come back to haunt man. We hardly notice natural resources such as air, water, soil and blue

# Appendix  Work Together to Build a Community of Shared Future for Mankind

sky when we have them. But we won't be able to survive without them. Industrialization has created material wealth never seen before, but it has also inflicted irreparable damage to the environment. We must not exhaust all the resources passed on to us by previous generations and leave nothing to our children or pursue development in a destructive way. Clear waters and green mountains are as good as mountains of gold and silver. We must maintain harmony between man and nature and pursue sustainable development.

We should pursue green, low-carbon, circular and sustainable way of life and production, advance the 2030 Agenda for Sustainable Development in a balanced manner and explore a model of sound development that ensures growth, better lives and a good environment. The Paris Agreement is a milestone in the history of climate governance. We must ensure this endeavor is not derailed. All parties should work together to implement the Paris Agreement. China will continue to take steps to tackle climate change and fully honor its obligations.

Swiss army knife embodies Swiss craftsmanship. When I first got one, I was amazed that it has so many functions. I cannot help thinking how wonderful it would be if an exquisite Swiss army knife could be made for our world. When there is a problem, we can use one of the tools on the knife to fix it. I believe that with unremitting efforts of the international community, such a knife can be made.

Ladies and gentlemen, friends, for us Chinese, China will do well only when the world does well, and vice versa. Many people are quite interested in what policies China will pursue, and we have heard various views. Here, I wish to give you an explicit answer.

**First, China remains unchanged in its commitment to uphold world peace.** Amity with neighbors, harmony without uniformity and peace are values cherished in the Chinese culture. *The Art of War*, a Chinese classic, begins with this observation, "The art of war is of vital importance to the State. It is a matter of life and death, a road to either survival or ruin. Hence it demands careful study." What it means is that every effort should be made to prevent a war and great caution must be exercised when it comes to fighting a war. For several millennia, peace has been in the blood of us Chinese and a part of our DNA.

Several centuries ago, China was strong and its GDP accounted for 30% of the global total. Even then, China was never engaged in aggression or expansion. In over 100 years after the 1840 Opium War, China suffered immensely from aggression, wars and chaos. Confucius said, "Do not do to others what you do not want others to do to you." We Chinese firmly believe that peace and stability is the only way to development and prosperity.

China has grown from a poor and weak country to the world's second largest economy not by committing military expansion or colonial plunder, but through the hard work of its people and our efforts to uphold peace. China will never waver in its pursuit of peaceful development. No matter how strong its economy grows, China will never seek hegemony, expansion or sphere of influence. History has borne this out and will continue to do so.

**Second, China remains unchanged in its commitment to pursue common development.** An old Chinese saying goes, when you reap fruits, you should remember the tree; when you drink water, you should remember its source. China's development has been possible because of the world, and China has contributed to the world's development. We will continue to pursue a win-win strategy of opening-up, share our development opportunities with other countries and welcome them aboard the fast train of China's development.

Between 1950 and 2016, China provided foreign countries with over 400 billion yuan of aid, and we will continue to increase assistance to others as its ability permits. Since the outbreak of the international financial crisis, China has contributed to over 30% of global growth each year on average. In the coming five years, China will import eight trillion US dollars of goods, attract 600 billion US dollars of foreign investment, make 750 billion US dollars of outbound investment, and Chinese tourists will make 700 million outbound visits. All this will bring more development opportunities to other countries.

China pursues a path of development in keeping with its national conditions. We always put people's rights and interests above everything else and have worked hard to advance and uphold human rights. China has met the basic living needs of its 1.3 billion-plus people and lifted over 700 million people out of poverty, which is a significant contribution to the global cause of human rights. The Belt and Road Initiative I put forward aims to achieve win-win and shared development. Over 100 countries and international organizations have supported the initiative, and a large number of early harvest projects have been launched. China supports the successful operation of the Asian Infrastructure Investment Bank and other new multilateral financial institutions in order to provide more public goods to the international community.

**Third, China remains unchanged in its commitment to foster partnerships.** China pursues an independent foreign policy of peace, and is ready to enhance friendship and cooperation with all other countries on the basis of the Five Principles of Peaceful Coexistence. China is the first country to make partnership-building a principle guiding state-to-state relations. It has formed partnerships of various forms with over 90 countries and regional organizations, and will build a circle of friends across the world.

China will endeavor to put in place a framework of relations with major powers featuring general stability and balanced growth. We will strive to build a new model of major country relations with the United States, a comprehensive strategic partnership of coordination with Russia, partnership for peace, growth, reform and among different civilizations with Europe, and a partnership of unity and cooperation with BRICS countries. China will continue to uphold justice and friendship and pursue shared interests, and boost pragmatic cooperation with other developing countries to achieve common development. We will further enhance

# Appendix  Work Together to Build a Community of Shared Future for Mankind

mutually beneficial cooperation with our neighbors under the principle of amity, sincerity, mutual benefit and inclusiveness. We will pursue common development with African countries in a spirit of sincerity, being result oriented, affinity and good faith. And we will elevate our comprehensive cooperative partnership with Latin America to a higher level.

**Fourth, China remains unchanged in its commitment to multilateralism.** Multilateralism is an effective way to preserve peace and promote development. For decades, the United Nations and other international institutions have made a universally recognized contribution to maintaining global peace and sustaining development.

China is a founding member of the United Nations and the first country to put its signature on the UN Charter. China will firmly uphold the international system with the UN as its core, the basic norms governing international relations embodied in the purposes and principles of the UN Charter, the authority and stature of the UN, and its core role in international affairs.

The China-UN Peace and Development Fund has been officially inaugurated. We will make funds available to peace and development oriented programs proposed by the UN and its agencies in Geneva on a priority basis. China's support for multilateralism will increase as the country continues to develop itself.

Ladies and gentlemen, friends, Geneva invokes a special memory to us. In 1954, Premier Zhou Enlai led a Chinese delegation to the Geneva Conference, and worked with the Soviet Union, the United States, the United Kingdom and France to seek political settlement of the Korean issue and a ceasefire in Indo-China. This demonstrated China's desire for peace and contributed Chinese wisdom to world peace. Since 1971 when China regained its lawful seat in the UN and began to return to international agencies in Geneva, China has gradually involved itself in disarmament, trade, development, human rights and social issues, putting forth Chinese proposals for the resolution of major issues and the making of important rules. In recent years, China has taken an active part in dialogs and negotiations on the Iranian nuclear issue, the Syrian issue and other hotspot issues, giving Chinese input to their political settlement. China applied to the International Olympic Committee to host both the summer and winter Olympic and Paralympic Games, and we have won the bids. In addition, we have gained endorsement from the International Union for Conservation of Nature for over a dozen applications for world natural heritage sites as well as world cultural and natural heritage sites. All this has presented Chinese splendor to the world.

Ladies and gentlemen, friends, the ancient Chinese believed that "one should be good at finding the laws of things and solving problems". Building a community of shared future is an exciting goal, and it requires efforts from generation after generation. China is ready to work with all the other UN member states as well as international organizations and agencies to advance the great cause of building a community of shared future for mankind.

On 28 January, we Chinese will celebrate the Chinese New Year, the Year of the Rooster. The rooster symbolizes bright prospects and auspiciousness. As a Chinese saying goes, the crow of the golden rooster heralds a great day for all. With that, I wish you all the very best and a very happy Chinese New Year! Thank you.